THE BUNKHOUSE CHRONICLES

FIELD NOTES FROM THE FIGURE 8 RANCH

CRAIG RULLMAN

SMOKE CREEK PRESS

Author photo, design of cover and book by Lynn Woodward.

First Smoke Creek Press Edition: 2019

Manufactured in the United States of America

Library of Congress Control Number: 2019902450

ISBN: 978-0-578-47091-7

Grateful acknowledgement is made to the following publications in which some of this work first appeared, sometimes in different forms: "The Anti-Millennial," *Range Magazine*; "For the River with Gratitude," *Northwest Steelheaders Magazine*; *The Nugget Newspaper*; "Outlaws and Indians," "Cool Water," "The Abundance Bomb," "The Digital Dictatorship," *Running Iron Report*, RunningIronReport.com; TheBunkhouseChronicle.com.

A very special thanks to *The Nugget Newspaper* in Sisters, Oregon.

SmokeCreekPress.com

First, for my wife Wendy

and then for our boys Buddy, Doc, Sam, Luke, and Remi

per saecula saeculorum

Contents

Foreword

Craig Rullman ambled out of the woods and into my newspaper office a few years back looking for work.

Mind you, he wasn't looking for a job; he was looking for work—by which I mean writing for the newspaper. Any ink-stained wretch will tell you that being a writer is something that you are, not just something that you do, and Craig was already a writer when he walked through the door. But there comes a time when the writer has to find a readership; otherwise he's merely journaling. Nothing wrong with that, but the engagement of a reader changes the game in important ways. If you take your craft seriously, it makes you hone it sharp. And you'd better have something to say and you'd better mean it, because you own it.

Before he showed up, I spent some time on his blog, The Bunkhouse Chronicle. My first thought was, "Damn! This guy can write!" My second thought was, "Damn, this guy's got something to say." I knew he had a columnist gig before he showed up for our "interview," which, if I recall correctly, was mostly talk about rifles and Cormac McCarthy. I knew by the time he left that we were going to be friends, for we are simpatico in the way we see and experience the world.

The actor Sam Elliott once said of the larger-than-life screenwriter and director John Milius: "He doesn't write for pussies and he doesn't write for women. He writes for men. 'Cause he's a man."

The same can be said of Craig Rullman. Now, this is not to say that women don't appreciate his work; they do. In fact, some of his most engaged readers are women—the kind that understand and appreciate men. For Rullman writes about eternal masculine verities—about strength, courage, honor, capability, love of beauty and a deep connection to landscape that comes not only from exploring it but from working on and in it.

He is writing about—and striving always to live—a manly life, in an age where speaking unironically of "manliness" invites scoffing derision. But the mead hall of Heorot was not filled with hip ironists, nor were the winter camps of the Rocky Mountain Fur Company or the ranks of the 2nd and 4th Marine Divisions on Saipan. We can ignore the snark and the pearl-clutching that vigorous writing about manly things may bring. Rullman is writing true things about things that will always be true, whether "society" values them or not.

This commentary-making is serious business, and like all serious business, it's also funny. Rullman is a true Romantic, in love with the wild, weird wonder of it all. And sometimes the humans are just so damn crazy you can't help but laugh. And sometimes they are so noble that you can't help but be moved to tears. I've seen Craig "go there"—to both places—and he takes his readers there with him. That's the work, right there.

So, here you hold a man's work—strong work that holds up: as Guy Clark sings, "the kind of stuff you don't hang on a wall." You don't leave it on a shelf, either. Pour a drink, stoke the fire and read on. 'Cause *damn* this guy can write—and he's got something to say.

—Jim Cornelius
author of *Warriors of the Wildlands*

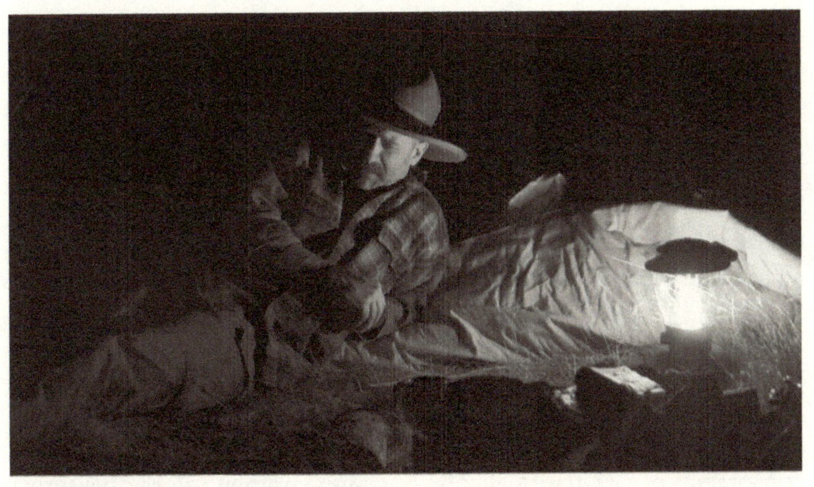

Outlaws & Indians: A Life Downstream

"When I think of our condition, my heart is heavy. I see men of my own race treated as outlaws and driven from country to country, or shot down like animals."

—Chief Joseph, Washington, DC, 1879

"If I knew for certain that a man was coming to my house with the conscious design of doing me good, I should run for my life."

—Henry David Thoreau

Some time ago the *New York Times* published a fine piece by Andrew McCarthy detailing his journey into the Omo Valley of southwestern Ethiopia. The remote Omo Valley, where human remains date back two and a half million years, is home to seven principle tribes who are now watching, defenseless, as their cultures of independence and self-reliance are shoved inexorably into disenfranchisement, dependence, and idle misery.

Like the sound of bugles and rifle fire coming from the next canyon over, there is a warning in this experience that we can all heed.

Patterns of life in the Omo have, for millennia, been predicated on the health and behavior of the Omo River. Pastoralists, the various tribes who live there have relied on the river's annual flooding to, by all accounts, sustainably maintain their crops of sorghum, maize, and beans, and to water the herds of domesticated livestock that supplement their diet. They have lived well, were satisfied with their lives, and neither looked for, nor needed, any outside help.

But all of that is now changing as the Ethiopian government and a consortium of international conglomerates complete work on a series of dams across the Omo River, creating downstream what *National Geographic* has called "a spreading humanitarian emergency that threatens to spawn conflict ... [and] is largely being met with silence from both the Ethiopian government and the international community. ... People are starving and dying."

The people of the Omo live far downstream from the dams, but more importantly they live far downstream from the sources of money and power that created them.

Those same pressures are at work for those of us living downstream from the power and money centers of Big America. The pressures are dressed up differently for us—neatly disguised by our camouflaging world of technology and super-abundance—but we too are increasingly dependent on, and dominated by, machinations of industry and government that operate far beyond any capacity we might have to meaningfully influence an outcome in our favor.

You can't fight City Hall, and you sure as hell can't fight Google. Or Amazon. Or Facebook. Or Apple.

What's most dangerous and disturbing about the intertwining of government programming with corporate scheming—like a couple of mating snakes—is that they ultimately work in concert to create, promote, and enforce utter dependency—either on the stuffs they produce or by means of the laws they pass. And we have no choice in the matter, really, because they are jealous creatures and ultimately whatever they may decide on—from pipelines to bullet trains through the family farm, from Alexa spying on us in our living rooms, to driverless cars and drones, is ultimately imposed on us whether we like it or not. Exploiting the marketable advantages of ease over concerns for sustainability is a winner and a money-maker every time. And, if necessary, they will do it by force.

As Addis Ababa and the World Bank are to the Omo Valley, so Washington, DC and corporate boardrooms are to River City. That is especially true if you happen to live in rural America, where objections are unlikely to register, and your vote is made meaningless by far-away cities where most of the people live.

It gets worse, naturally. As the Omo River has failed to flood with the creation of the dams, so has a new government policy of "villagisation" taken hold, wherein Omo Valley peoples are stripped of their ability to raise their own food, subsequently lose their self-reliance and independence, and are finally force-marched into displacement camps.

As usual, those who go passively onto the reservation are left starving and destitute, while those who resist are outlawed or eventually killed in order to make more room for ecologically ruinous hydro-electric schemes and enormous, internationally controlled plantations of sugarcane, cotton, rice, and palm oil.

The script now playing out in the Omo has, from Africa to South America, from Australia to Canada, been what we traditionally held up as the progress of Western civilization in the service of mankind.

And it has provided unparalleled luxury and long periods of security, even as we destroyed every model of sustainable agriculture along the way, murdered or enslaved entire populations, and ultimately quashed any notions of independence and self-reliance for the sake of comfort.

In *The Unsettling of America*, novelist, poet, and ecologist Wendell Berry offers us this:

> *"If there is any law that has been consistently operative in American history, it is that the members of any established people or group or community sooner or later become 'redskins'—that is, they become the designated victims of an utterly ruthless, officially sanctioned and subsidized exploitation. The colonists who drove off the Indians came to be intolerably exploited by their imperial governments. And that alien imperialism was thrown off only to be succeeded by a domestic version of the same thing; the class of independent small farmers who fought the war of independence has been exploited by, and recruited into, the industrial society until by now it is almost extinct. Today, the most numerous heirs to the farmers of Lexington and Concord are the little groups scattered all over the country whose names begin with 'Save': Save our Land, Save the Valley, Save Our Mountains, Save Our Streams, Save Our Farmland. As so often before, these are designated victims—people without official sanction, often without official friends, who are struggling to preserve their places, their values, and their lives as they know them and prefer to live them against the agencies of their own government, which are using their own tax moneys against them."*

Take a drive through any American Indian reservation, inner-city housing project, the coal seams of Appalachia, or enjoy a toxic stroll across the potato fields of Idaho if you want to see the finer fruits of subsidized exploitation, and its consequent government-enforced dependency.

"The first casualties of the exploitive revolution," Berry writes, "are character and community," which is probably the finest observation yet of the intellectual poverty, financial recklessness, extreme lawlessness, ecological destruction, and spiritual vacuity we see all around us. We fool only ourselves if we believe that in our comfortably modern, convenient, and eminently exploitable middle-class worlds we are somehow immune to outcomes like those faced by people in the Omo Valley.

The injuries to character and community Berry notes are real, lasting, and highly visible. They are the manifest symptoms of a commodity rich and yet spiritually diseased and corporatized culture that has invaded our better judgment under the banner of the "growth economy." Worse, seen on such a grand and pervasive scale, those symptoms are also historically reliable indicators of an empire whose foundation is rotting, and whose finest days are probably in the rearview mirror.

Post World War II, manufacturing in the United States has been offshored and replaced by behemoth, mysterious, and unaccountable service corporations such as Amazon and Google whose power, like a vine of strangling kudzu, outstrips even that of our elected government.

In the case of Amazon, even the corporate name is suggestive of the "counterfeit paradise of South America," a place full of vibrant life and activity where one can easily starve to death.

As Candice Millard wrote so evocatively in *The River of Doubt*:

> *"The rain forest was not a garden of easy abundance, but precisely the opposite. Its quiet, shaded halls of leafy opulence were not a sanctuary, but rather the greatest natural battlefield anywhere on the planet, hosting an unremitting and remorseless fight for survival that occupied every single one of its inhabitants, every minute of every day."*

The synthetic Amazon, one can't help but think, is a first cousin to the natural one, whose many ways to kill are likewise camouflaged by seduction—the patterns and temptations of ease and convenience.

Amazon's recent move into the food business—by acquiring Whole Foods Corporation—ought to scare the daylights out of those of us living downstream. By injecting itself into the control and distribution of foods, Amazon's corporate motives highlight the average citizen's utter dependency on unaccountable, centrally planned, and egregiously unreliable corporate behemoths for the sources even of our own nutrition.

If you aren't actively learning how to grow a garden or secure your own sources of protein, you probably should be. Because if there is ever a break in the food-supply chain you can be certain that it won't be Jeff Bezos et al. who are going hungry.

But *you* probably will be. And just like the people of the Omo, when you can't feed yourself, or your family, you are easily manipulated and exploitable, and will soon find yourself stripped of everything else you hold dear—including your human dignity.

Victor Davis Hanson, in his excellent treatise *The Fragility of Complex Societies,* wrote:

> *"In a wider sense, America's strength has always been found in the self-reliant, highly individualist, even eccentric citizen. ... We need these cranky independent people, if only as a minority to remind the rest of us who are plugged into huge conglomerations, both private and public, for our wages and sustenance, that there are dangers with reliance on hierarchy, centralized government, and high density—which, well beyond fragility, inevitably results in groupthink, fad, and cultural uniformity."*

What Hanson proposes as our greatest cultural strength—those independent, cranky, and eccentric citizens—are often precisely the people we need most, but as a result of all that independence they are also most often the first to find themselves turned into outlaws and Indians. That remains true even as we are making fewer of them to begin with, and even as those who manage to reach a majority are chased onto the reservation by an army of relentlessly groupthink hashtag soldiers and social justice warriors.

Hanson writes:

> *"Today's popular culture knows Facebook well, but does one in a thousand know that a bee is necessary for an almond to set, or what a piston and cylinder are, or the difference between a southern and northern storm? I once asked my students to explain the winter solstice, not just the astronomy of it, but what such a date portended in terms of work, culture, and mindset. It was in the 1990s, and my favorite answer was, 'She was a rap singer, Sister Solstice that mouthed off too much.'"*

This sort of undergraduate intellectual lassitude shows up in the trends of our national conversations too, which mostly happen on television or the internet, and where they often devolve into incomprehensible shouting matches moderated by the media lawn-jockeys at CNN or Fox—equally unwatchable spectacles of corporate self-aggrandizement and binary political shilling.

As one example of the collapse of our once-famous American self-reliance—under what is now, in many states, legislated dependency—I offer the example of a 911 call for service I responded to as a police officer in California. After I had arrived the reporting party met me at the door and explained that her emergency was a ten-year old—a profane, obese, filthy lump of humanity I could see brachiating around the living room behind her. The problem? He was refusing to go to school.

Wendell Berry cites a related and easily observable phenomenon. "Our model citizen," he writes, "is a sophisticate who before puberty understands how to produce a baby, but who at the age of thirty will not know how to produce a potato."

Admirably, Berry restrains his alarm, leaving the rest of us to study the import and impact of this phenomenon, a true-enough generational pox which can only hasten the demise of a once fine dream: the dream of a free nation inhabited by reasonably self-reliant, self-sufficient, and therefore independent peoples similarly endowed with the capacity and desire to defend those ideals against the extremely agile and powerful forces that would exploit and control them. Those forces have always included the government and corporate boardrooms.

Frederick Russell Burnham, who served as a scout and worked tirelessly as an entrepreneur in the age of colonial expansion and exploitation, came early to understand the long-range dangers of his own pursuits:

> *"That great strength and bulwark of the 19th-century civilization, vested rights and inheritance, will be a prime factor in its complete undoing. But ... when the old order of things has passed away as a dream of the night, will we rebuild on a better and truer basis? Being an optimist, I think yes."*

Sadly, the current model of successful citizenry doesn't seem to mind losing their freedoms and independence, or even notice that it's a problem. Which is a direct result of allowing ourselves to be herded onto retail sales and marketing reservations where our every waking moment is subject to increasing, rather than decreasing, dependency on the modern version of Indian Agents: WalMart, Target, and Starbucks.

Decades of that mindset has, Berry writes, left us "... frustratingly helpless and ignorant in regard to basic human skills—growing food, maintaining a home, caring for and educating children, promoting friendship and cooperation, facing illness and death—as well as financially dependent on other specialists."

One result of this dependency is now clearly observable in politics, where virtually any celebrity, regardless of their qualification, has a legitimate prospect of being elected into public office—and even of becoming the President of the United States.

Those of us making a deliberate choice to resist these pernicious influences in our lives had better accept that we will, eventually, be made into outlaws and Indians. Our insistence on remaining reasonably self-reliant—and vigorously defending the benefits of an independent mind—is ultimately threatening to those who would exploit us for profit and notions of progress.

But it is never enough to point at the horizon and declare that a storm is coming. Far better, one thinks, to prepare for its arrival and to safeguard our natural rights in advance. Which is a thing we do well by reducing our trust in, and therefore our dependency on, predatory corporations and retail representation in government. In the long term, we build stout resilience when we devote our energies to local communities and local economies—where our voices, our money, and our votes may still matter.

And perhaps most importantly, we can help keep our children out of the intellectual stockades of the future by teaching them to value things that last, to fix things that break, and to consider each innovation with an eye on conservation of the resources we rely on. We can arm them for meaningful resistance in the long struggle to preserve their independence by teaching them to think—rather than merely feel—their way through the howling winds and utter darkness of the approaching cultural storm.

Under the Volcano

Yesterday, encouraged by the bluest skies, I bravely opened the door to our "shop." The shop— where I like to futz and putter and try to make things, or fix things, or think about things—had become a desultory crypt of neglect.

That's my fault. It's been something of a challenging winter thus far—three feet of snow and temperatures regularly dropping below zero—and I've tried to conserve and focus my energies on more pressing concerns, which means that sometimes, more often than I would like to admit, I've tromped through the snow, opened the shop door, tossed something in, and then closed the door.

But there it was: a big, dark, yawning disaster of disorganization. Fuel cans, battery chargers, scraps of lumber, piles of hunting gear, tools in all the wrong places—a landfill of my own making. And now it was staring back at me, punctuated by the grating irritation of the talk radio I leave on inside because I believe—with zero scientific evidence—that mice are united in their hatred of *The Lars Larson Show,* and will seek other accommodations.

So, I went to work. And for some reason—probably because our own volcanic peaks were standing up so perfectly in the rarified sunlight—I started thinking about Malcolm Lowry's excellent novel, *Under the Volcano.*

If you've not read it, the book follows the last day on earth of a British diplomat in the town of Quauhnahuac, Mexico. It is a difficult, sometimes sordid drama, and plays out to its tragic end under the quiet eyes of two ancient and enormous volcanoes.

The volcanoes are important to the story because they lend the perspective of time. They suggest durability, and wisdom—there is nothing happening below that they haven't seen before—and they are a reminder that the hard hunt for the longer truths often evades us down here, in our little shops and villages, as we scheme and muscle through the daily Sturm und Drang of an increasingly synthetic 21st century.

It was fitting enough, then, to think of that book while deciding why I should need an entire drawer full of rusty pipe reamers, or how a box full of .280 Ackley handloads—missing for several months—ended up with a jar of wrecked paintbrushes—all buried under a pair of old hip-waders. It was fitting, I think, because we live in the shadow our own geologic sentinels. Mountains that, when the sun is out and shining on all that snowy transcendence, we can meditate on just long enough to experience the sublime frisson of our own impermanence.

That should—but mostly doesn't—spur us into a different way of thinking about things. It might even, in a best-case scenario, cause us to think differently about how we intend to manage ourselves during the Cold Civil War we are apparently descending into.

We can learn a lot from just looking up. There is an old story of a Japanese watercolorist who sat outside each morning, staring through the mists at a mountain across the valley. He did this every morning for decades before he ever tried to paint it. And when he finally did paint the mountain, it was a masterpiece finished in minutes. Or so the story goes, and the larger part of me wants very much to believe it is true.

True or not, it was not the story in our shop. Some part of me toyed with the idea of just staring through the mist of the mess a little longer, on the outside chance it would organize itself, and that the great invisible Lord of the Volcanic Cascades would somehow find pleasure with my conviction. But I don't have those kinds of powers, or whatever that magic is called, and so it was back to unraveling the mystery of how, over the years, I have managed to collect so many combination locks, without recording—anywhere—the combinations, and why they were all in an old ammo can marked: Tape and Glue.

The volcanoes in Lowry's book are monoliths. They are the Romantics' notion of negative capability. They say everything by saying nothing. As do our own. They aren't even noticeably bemused by the strange and grinding duplicities we put on display each day, and that we seem to be insisting on. They just watch. And listen.

It occurred to me, as I performed a kind of kabuki dance with the ponderously heavy and awkward bag containing our wall tent, grotesquely dragging it from one corner of the shop to another, that the vows of silence adopted by various religious orders are increasingly understandable.

What, really, is there to say?

Walt Whitman, who was ahead of most curves in life, wrote about an alternative, and offered a kind of salve for the sharpened dilemmas of modern duplicity that keep stabbing me in the side. He wrote: "Do I contradict myself? Very well then, I contradict myself. I am large, I contain multitudes." So that's another way to go, if we can keep our multitudes honest. I don't know if we can. For certain, the mountains won't care one way or the other.

In the meantime, down here under the mountains, I was able to get the shop arranged in some kind of working order. It took some effort—and discipline—but I persevered to inject some logic back into the equation, and that kind of work is always its own reward. But this morning, naturally, in a rush to be somewhere else, and forgetting everything I had so laboriously learned, I opened the door, tossed in a bag of ice melt, and abruptly closed the door again.

The Abundance Bomb

We have—my apologies to the late George Carlin—a lot of stuff. The great successes of the industrial revolution, the service economy, and the continuing dominance of Western civilization in areas of innovation, production, and scale, has been to create societies simply dripping with abundance. Across the board, we are drowning in commodities—from foodstuffs to kitchen appliances, from television shows to tractors. We have so much stuff, in fact, that our landfills are overflowing, the oceans (and I've seen this while transiting the Pacific on Navy warships) contain vast floating continents of trash, and we throw out an estimated sixty billion tons of fresh produce each year. Even the poorest among us, the homeless and destitute, routinely possess cell phones.

This abundance, this giant ticking bomb, is the result of steadfast belief in the growth economy, hyper-efficient economies of scale, and the seduction of nearly every one of us into the role of dedicated—one might say blindly addicted—consumer. But there is a flipside to the consumerism that has continued to drive innovation and the ease and comfort it has brought to our lives: ultimately, our willingness to be indoctrinated and manipulated—to be persuaded by the Jedis of marketing and advertisement that we have a need for almost anything—is wracked with the consequences of exploitation.

It also creates a moral bind. The ease and convenience of cell phones (and many other products) trumps any meaningful concerns about how the minerals for those devices are mined—often by forced child labor. Nevermind the scarcity of the resources needed to make billions of phones, and the preservation of those resources for later generations. It seems much more important that we have our cell phones right now, and anyway, screw the nine-year-old kid in the Congo basin digging by hand with an AK barrel in his back—he should have a better government if he doesn't want that to happen to him. I've heard that claim, or related defenses, made more than once, by otherwise moral and reliable people who are willing to reject outright the consideration of these and similar moral conundrums when the questions challenge their natural rights to abundance. And no one is more ferocious than a sad, lonely, consumerist American faced with the suggestion that his insistence on immediate gratification as a natural right—the just fruits of American hegemony—also makes him a hypocrite.

It is not my purpose here to argue that advancements in technology, medicine, and other key areas of life are always bad things. To my mind, they merely *are*; time will ultimately judge if they were wise. Time will sort out whether or not sacrificing the sustainable legacy of small farms to the industrialized behemoths of agribusiness conglomerates was ultimately a smart move. One doesn't think so, but there are plenty of mouths to feed the world over. And certainly we all enjoy the notion that if we were to develop a toothache we can go see a dentist, rather than sit in a tipi during the Moon of the Cracking Trees, chewing on whang leather and listening to the incantations of a medicine man for distraction from the pain.

So it isn't the moral questions I'm trying to resolve. Certainly I'm trying to highlight moral aspects of our consumerism, but I don't have a claim to righteousness and I'm not pushing one on you. Rather, I would rather focus on the much more personal questions of individual and community need, considered in the broader perspective, with one eye on designing a life around wanting, and therefore needing, less stuff, and the other eye on learning ways to persuade those whose only—and it is trained from birth—response to abundance is to angrily demand more, more, and even more.

The film actor Paul Newman—and I don't normally turn to actors for great wisdom—while speaking to *The New York Times* in 1990, had this poignant thing to say about our consumerist addictions:

> *"We're a throw-away society, aren't we? We throw away everything. We never even try to fix things—we throw them away, we destroy things—appliances that break, old buildings because they're old, we throw away relationships that aren't exactly what we thought they'd be, we throw away wives, husbands, marriages."*

We have so much, the abundance of our success so virtually surrounds us, and yet we are among the least satisfied, ardently unhappy, and in some ways spiritually destitute people on the planet.

Since 1957, the median income of Americans has risen some eighty-five percent, while the average assessment of our own happiness has *decreased* by five percent. That's no accident.

There are two axioms to bear in mind when celebrating the successes of our growth economy and innovation in our time, both of them offered by Wendell Berry in his masterwork, *The Gift of Good Land*: First: "... manufacturers profit most from increases of scale, not community stability." Second: "No new machine is ever introduced that will help the existing community to survive."

The models of modern farming—and farming is always a good place to start because eating well is the bedrock of health and happiness—are designed to disrupt and eliminate small farmers, or at least have as their ultimate consequence the annihilation of small farmers—a vision we cling to—this nation of small farmers—even as it increasingly devolves into mythology.

There are seductive reasons to make a Super Bowl halftime commercial (complete with a moving voiceover from Paul Harvey) purporting to celebrate the American family farm. But in the end that commercial, like most commercials, is a well-dressed and sentimental lie selling things, like pickups, to people who live in the utter dependency of a cookie-cutter modern suburb. In farming, as elsewhere, the introduction of new machines, or technologies, exploits us by carefully creating and nurturing reliance and dependence upon the products as the price of ease and convenience—and an easier sale is almost never made.

Berry cites the example of the Amish farms:

> *"Surely our nation would be healthier if it contained several million such farms. And yet Amish farms have received virtually no attention from students of agriculture—the reason being, I think, that these farms are more profitable to the farmers than to those corporations whose livelihood has been the ruin of farmers. They consume small quantities of chemicals and commercial fertilizers; they use simple machines that last as long as machines ought to last; they use virtually no petroleum; they do not look upon indebtedness as a desirable temporary condition, much less a desirable permanent one; they grow their own sustenance.*
>
> *"But take, say, fifteen eighty-acre Amish farms and join them together in the ownership of an 'agribusinessman,' who will get rid of the livestock, take out the fences, buy the large machinery necessary to farm on a big scale, and plant all twelve hundred acres in corn or corn and beans. Health will decline in everything from the soil to the community ... This farmer-as-agribusinessman will*

> *be a life-long extravagant consumer of everything he needs, from fuel to fertilizer, from credit to extension courses in 'stress management'. He will be a good citizen of the economy. But whether he knows it or not, and sooner or later he will know it, this economy proposes to ruin him, as it has ruined millions of others, and sell him out to a bigger agribusinessman who wants to 'handle' 2400 acres and help the economy even more."*

What is true about all of this in farming is also true in virtually every other aspect of our consumer economy. Who doesn't yearn for a doctor who makes house calls, and isn't enslaved to the corporate medicine and insurance rackets?

We suffer, and I think it is an acquired illness, from terminal shortsightedness in how we choose to live on and nurture the things of this planet. That illness leads directly to the now obvious symptoms of a diseased culture: mass shootings, rotting public schools, endless overseas wars and entanglements, disingenuous politics, endless racial strife, inveterate poverty and homelessness, ecological madness—and it even presents in less obvious ways, as in our approach to maintenance of the national debt.

Yet we go on assuming that the producers of each innovation and latest "must have" product have only the best intentions in mind for consumers. That's true even after the widespread use of DDT and the string of catastrophes it caused, after asbestos wreaked its brand of havoc across the world, after Roundup was discovered to cause cancer, and even after Teflon chemicals developed by DuPont have somehow leached into the bloodstreams of Americans across the continent.

New products, such as the thousand-dollar iPhone, are rolled out with planned pageantry and presented to the consumer in ritualized events, like the consecration of a saint meant for us to worship. And the subsequently intense product-worship can even result in riots, like those we see each year during the Thanksgiving Black Friday phenomenon.

And yet we ride away on these waves of innovation with precious little focus on either their immediate or downstream consequences.

In *The Conundrum of Consumption,* Alan Thein Durning wrote: "Thus many of us in the consumer society have a sense that our world of plenty is somehow hollow—that, hoodwinked by a consumerist culture, we have been fruitlessly attempting to satisfy with material things what are essentially social, psychological, and spiritual needs."

Facebook—which I use, and have written critically about elsewhere—is one of the finer examples of our hollowed-out, hoodwinked modern life. Not long ago, I was condemned by an *angry reader* for a newspaper column I wrote about the finer dangers of Facebook. This gentleman, who was probably well-intentioned, called the piece a "rant against connectivity."

It most certainly was. With good reason. And I will let one of the founders of Facebook illustrate why. Sean Parker, the founding president of Facebook, recently gave this eye-opening interview into Facebook's intentional design. The emphases are mine:

> *"When Facebook was getting going, I had these people who would come up to me and they would say, 'I'm not on social media.' And I would say, 'OK. You know, you will be.' And then they would say, 'No, no, no. I value my real-life interactions. I value the moment. I value presence. I value intimacy.' And I would say, ...* ***'We'll get you eventually.'*** *...*
>
> *... I don't know if I really understood the consequences of what I was saying, because [of] the unintended consequences of a network when it grows to a billion or two billion people and ...* ***it literally changes your relationship with society, with each other ... It probably interferes with productivity in weird ways. God only knows what it's doing to our children's brains.*** *...*
>
> *... The thought process that went into building these applications,*

> *Facebook being the first of them, ... was all about: '**How do we consume as much of your time and conscious attention as possible?**' ...*
>
> *... And that means that **we need to sort of give you a little dopamine hit every once in a while,** because someone liked or commented on a photo or a post or whatever. And that's going to get you to contribute more content, and that's going to get you ... more likes and comments. ...*
>
> *... It's a social-validation feedback loop ... exactly the kind of thing that a hacker like myself would come up with, because you're **exploiting a vulnerability in human psychology**. ...*
>
> *... The inventors, creators—it's me, it's Mark [Zuckerberg], it's Kevin Systrom on Instagram, it's **all of these people—understood this consciously. And we did it anyway.**"*

At least as revealed in this interview, very little, if any, thought was given to the downstream consequences. The product was made, marketed, and eagerly consumed by billions of users as the next great thing. It also became, in many ways, a replacement for the usual requirement of thinking before speaking, and even the briefest tour of the Facebook landscape reveals a populace steeped in gloom, conspiracy, meme-think, bubble-gum politics, and the utterly inane behavior of endlessly gyrating pop stars. In many cases it is similar to being detained in a kind of uber-sentimental nightmare—a bad-jokes, stupid-thoughts, greeting-card ante-chamber to hell.

The most intelligent thing I've heard said about Facebook came at a machine-gun shoot in Arizona, from a freelance writer and editor who was also there covering the event. "Facebook," he said, "should only ever be a one-way conversation." And he meant, if he was being honest, that he only uses Facebook to market his writing and business.

For many of us, these quotes from Mr. Parker are not revelations—

we've suspected as much for some time—but they are admissions of a deliberate strategy aimed at mind control. Which should probably be terrifying. It is startling to realize that American consumers would line up, willingly and with unrestrained enthusiasm, to indulge in the ease and convenience of a product intentionally designed to control their minds.

This is exceptionally true because we don't—and will never—know to what ends the platform is ultimately being used, or by whom, as demonstrated by Russian use of Facebook memes and marketing strategies in an attempt to influence the 2016 presidential election. And it is controlled minds—either by consumerism, religious fundamentalism, and/or unquestioned belief in the immortal virtues of a growth economy—that are so difficult to persuade that the voices they hear are actually screams coming up from the bottom of the well.

Jerry Mander (yes, his real name) wrote in *The Walling of Awareness* that "What we see, hear, touch, taste, smell, feel and understand about the world has been processed for us. Our experiences of the world can no longer be called direct, or primary. They are secondary, mediated experiences." Nowhere is the secondary, mediated experience more apparent than in the world of Facebook and, according to Mr. Parker, it is entirely deliberate.

We have options, and most of them are personal. No single person among us is likely to persuade some four hundred million Americans and those billions more across the globe that our addiction to consumerism is ultimately dangerous and counter-productive to independence of thought and action. Like any faith, it becomes a personal commitment. What's required is a concerted effort to fill in the hollow places we know exist because we can see and feel them, to address the planned obsolescence of our goods—and even our own lives—by making more careful and deliberate choices, by exercising options anchored firmly in family and local community, and to steadfastly refuse to be harried into a political corner by irrelevant party platforms and the zealots who defend them. The once admirable American political system has devolved into a marketing and consumerist free-for-all, utterly devoid of meaning, a kind of freak show capable only of trotting out the worst possible candidates for public office.

Alice Walker wrote, in her poem "We Alone":

> *We alone can devalue gold*
> *by not caring*
> *if it falls or rises in the marketplace.*
> *Wherever there is gold*
> *there is a chain, you know,*
> *and if your chain is gold*
> *so much the worse*
> *for you.*

We can avoid the explosion of the abundance bomb in our lives by changing out, consciously and conscientiously, those things on which we place value. And it is a big, powerful bomb. The people who built it, and defend it, have much to lose if it is ever finally defused, but we have everything to gain by climbing down into the crater and getting to work with a screwdriver and wire cutters. We win if we go down there next to the beast with our tools, like the Indian sapper Kip from Ondaatje's excellent novel *The English Patient*, and set out to deliberately disarm the pernicious and empty insistence on blind consumerism and models of a growth economy that ultimately destroy exactly what they are pretending to preserve and enhance.

Jim Dodge, in *Living by Life*, had this to say:

> *"We spend more time posturing than we do getting it on. In short, American culture has become increasingly gutless and barren in our lifetimes, and the political system little more than a cover for an economics that ravages the planet and its people for the financial gain of very few. It seems almost a social obligation to explore alternatives. Our much heralded standard of living hasn't done much for the quality of our daily lives; the glut of commodities, endlessly hurled at us out of the vast commodity spectacle, is just*

> *more shit on the windshield. ... Our only claim to dignity is trying our best to do what we think is right, to put some heart in it, some soul, flower and root. We're going to fall on our asses a lot, founder on our pettiness and covetousness and sloth, but at least there is the effort, and that's surely better than being just another quivering piece of the national cultural Jell-O."*

The effort against becoming a wiggling bowl of Jell-O, like most efforts of enduring value, start at home. They start with an insistence on remaining, wherever possible, independent in our thoughts, and in our hearts, which ultimately allows us to remain, if we have the courage, independent in our actions.

Independence remains the most powerful tool at our disposal. The cluster bombs of commodity dependence, mental and physical slavery to consumerism, and the cultural sociopathy that are the inevitable result, have fallen all around us. But if we care enough, and spend the time to identify them, we can chart a course that runs deliberately, happily, and safely, right through the middle of them all.

Lashed to the Mast

If you were ever lucky enough to live out on the Great Sagebrush Sea, like I was during a certain vanishing era, you might have enjoyed a slice of old Americana in perhaps the rarest of ways: trailing cattle and working horses.

The outback was, in those days—and still is to some degree—a kind of underworld, a parallel universe, richly populated with characters and stories both real and imagined. Most folks, I think it's fair to say, travel through the desert without much pause. They might admire some dazzling vista, or stop at a favorite greasy spoon, or even camp for a night or two on a lonely butte, but mostly they pour coal to the fire and yawn at the empty miles.

But there is a real-enough daily life out there on the big oceans of desert, and it was out there that I was blessed to spend some time with a real American legend, Len Babb.

I first started hearing about Len, and his magnificent saddles, in the long ago, when I rode the big empty with another legendary buckaroo named Bert Lambert. Bert was a Mescalero Apache, up from New Mexico, who could rope a tick off a dog's ass at a dead run, and whose stories were so outlandish, so outrageous, and so thoroughly questionable, that I actually started writing them down. I have an entire notebook I titled, way back then: The Bert Lambert Lies.

An example from the notebook: "Bert said today that he once rode an ostrich somewhere near Christmas Valley, up in Oregon. 'Not much buck,' he said, 'But they sure do run fast.'"

Imagine my surprise then, all of these years later, when I finally met Len Babb in person, and was enjoying a fine lunch prepared by his wife Gloria, and learned that so many of Bert's imaginative stories of mayhem were actually true.

What makes Len Babb a hall-of-famer in the buckaroo world is not just his wonderful artwork, his appreciation for fine horsemanship, or his work for storied ranches such as The Padlock, out in Wyoming, or the ZX here in Oregon. It's the longevity of his career. Most buckaroo careers look more like mine did: a deep, and altogether too short, dive into the depths. With wages stuck forever in the 19th century, that's really just a matter of economics, and very few ever accomplish what Len and Gloria did, let alone raise six children.

Sipping root beer under the wind chimes on his porch—Len told me he had real beer, but we agreed the interview might go awry—I asked him the obvious question: Why did you stick it out all these years?

"Because I love it," he said. Simple as that. And it filled me with a certain hard-edged, inexplicable personal remorse such that I couldn't find a way to the next part of the interview. Len, mercifully, gave me an out. "Bills are bills," he said, and then told a joke about his friend

John Adamson, who was being interviewed by photographers out documenting the life. They were curious about the changes John had seen in his decades as a working buckaroo. "Well," John told them, "the wages are the same."

I've long held a thought in my head, maybe too simplistic, that as soon as they start paving the roads, a mostly unexplored, unfamiliar and wide-open chunk of country is more or less finished. The mystery runs all out of it. At least for the folks that once enjoyed it for its demanding, and beautiful, remoteness. That's possibly nostalgic, but when you've lived mostly horseback on a country, and learned its moods that way, there is more than a bit of remorse to see how easy it suddenly is to get from here to there.

We commiserated, just a little bit, on how the big ranches are breaking up and disappearing with increasing speed. We talked about how the country was filling up with people, "settling up" in Len's words, and I mentioned, perhaps too bitterly, that "We can't stop what's coming."

Len just smiled: "You can't even slow it down," he said. "Just be glad you got in on a piece of it. That's the way I look at it."

One of the things I love about Len, and it's been true of so many of the real buckaroos of his generation, is how genuinely open-minded he is. "I never wanted anybody telling me what to do, and I never wanted to boss anyone," he said.

A man like Len can say that without irony, and offer his life as proof, which makes him rare enough in the world.

In his handbuilt log studio, which could easily stand in for a perfect bunkhouse on any ranch I've ever known, Len has an old FA Meaney saddle sitting on a rack. It has the WT mark on it, meaning it was built in the Wyoming Territory, probably in the 1860s, and most likely in Cheyenne, by Frank Meaney—another legend of the cowboy underworld. He has a collection of beautifully crafted rawhide reatas—which he still ropes with—beautiful enough to make a sadsack towny like myself cry out loud. He has a pair of big-rowelled spurs that his father traded off of a Sioux Indian back in Wyoming, a rack of muzzle-loaders that he has killed bucks with, and a single skylight that throws the heavenly desert light down onto his canvas while he works.

Winters, he sits by the big wood stove in the middle of the room, turning beeswax into beautifully sculpted horses.

He has a buckaroo's hands, lithe and precise, soft in a horse's mouth, steady for brushstrokes on canvas, but hard enough in the right places to knock a rude man into next Wednesday.

Len focuses his work on the early years of the open West. "After the automobile came in, the glamor of cowboying went out the window," he said. "I did a lot of good cowboying, but not like you wanna draw pictures of. People come around and say, 'Well, Len, I guess you get a lot of ideas out there,' and I tell 'em I really don't because what would you paint? Somebody getting out of a horse trailer? An old black cow staring at you?"

Len wants his paintings to sell, and they have, and I'm confident he's on the edge of something much bigger, once the world finds him, but that isn't why he does it. "The people I've associated with could count all their money without taking their hands out of their pockets," he said. Which is the same pleasing grit a buckaroo reaches for when he is moving three hundred pairs alone, miles from anywhere, up-canyon in a storm blowing sideways. Money isn't the reason a man signs up for that kind of thing. It's passion, a deep, abiding, unwavering passion.

My own grandfather begged me not to go out into the desert. "You'll never have a pot to piss in, or a window to throw it out of," he said. He was right about that, and I knew it, but we both knew that it in my case it wouldn't matter. You either hear the siren song or you don't. And if you look out into the desert and hear it, and chase it down, lashed to the mast like Ulysses, it alters forever the way you see the world.

What informs Len Babb's art, his drawings, paintings, and sculptures, is that siren song. He's heard it his entire life, since the day his father moved the family from South Dakota into Glendo, Wyoming, hauling one truckfull of horses, and one full of cattle, stopping every now and then to pour water on the over-heating engines.

And then Charlie Russell came into Len's life and threw gas on the fire.

Len Babb is a man I am honored to have shared a few laughs with on a beautiful desert afternoon. He has heard those beautiful sirens of the outback singing in his ear, been lashed to the mast, and it is likely that he has sailed as close to the shores of Titan as a man in the modern era ever will.

The Sweetwater Brewing Company

A few years ago, after losing my grandparents, my dad, and our son, in a rapid cascade of debilitating blows, I needed to get away. *Badly.* I was working sixty-to-seventy-hour weeks as a narcotics detective, a notorious and occasionally dangerous grind of surveillance and door kicking, and what little time I had left was devoted to sorting out the detritus of the recent dead, comforting the living, and taking on responsibility for my disabled uncle.

It was a tough time, with a tremendous learning curve, and I simply hadn't been afforded the space I needed to digest the tornado of change that had ripped through our lives, let alone to properly mourn the loss of those who were giants and superheroes in my life. After one particularly difficult week, I commuted home from a demanding surveillance operation in southern Los Angeles, grinding through the stop-and-go traffic of LA, the rush-hour 405, in a near homicidal pique, intensely over-pressured, exhausted, juggling a police radio and two cell phones, and yearning desperately, angrily, for some other life, some other place, some permanent relief from the relentless and plugging donkeywork that had become my life. I arrived home, hours later, supercharged with attitude, the aimless distemper that inevitably results when there is simply too much demand and not enough character to meet it.

Enter Wendy. I have made some very bad decisions in this life, and live with those consequences still. But I will go to my grave knowing that I married exactly once, and exactly right. When I came home that night, a pure and fuming pile of toxic waste, my bride, who by some undeserved but precise endowment of the cosmos is my perfect match, ordered me to get away. Now. With a long and satisfying hug, she insisted that I pack my gear and head for the mountains, ordering up the perfect cure like room service. There is no expression of gratitude in our language expansive enough to capture my appreciation for this miracle of a woman, and I mourn for those who live without a similar gift in their own lives.

And fortunately, for me, when the order from Miss Wendy came, I knew precisely where I needed to go: the home country, the eastern High Sierras, where my own dreams of life took shape, where no flora, no fauna, no iteration of human being was entirely strange. I needed something from those jagged peaks, a private vision, a discreet and personal destination. I wanted to climb some nameless mountain, to endure designed and deliberate rigor in a type of post-modern vision quest.

I would never have the stamina, or the marrow, or the *from-birth* cultural guidance of a Lakota warrior sitting in a Black Hills eagle pit, but I could sweat myself to a ridgeline high above the mendacious world and create a ritual of my own, a ceremony to accommodate hard loss. What I had in mind required suffering and sacrifice, deliberation and economy, a commitment to accept the damages of loss, to purge the anguish and to emerge stronger than when I started.

I was in luck, for this place was available. My friend Don Berinati owns a cabin near Bridgeport, California, a place he built with his own gifted hands, considerable foresight, and a conscientious study of the strictly necessary. Don lived at the "Sweetwater Brewing Company" for many years, season after season, through violent winter storms, through wildfires, through long and cool summer nights, the sky salted with stars most people never see anymore, alone with his books, a good fire, and a good dog.

By trade a builder, in winter Don would ski into and out of the cabin, braving mountain lions and bears—very real threats in that remote place—dragging a sled with his possibles and groceries. He would sometimes make this trek at night, through high winds and swirling snows, a long, dark slog and an impressive feat anywhere in the wild world.

I came to know Don in Reno, Nevada, where we both studied writing under Gailmarie Pahmeier, the famed poet and teacher. Don and I became friends, meeting for "Any Silver Coin" beer nights at the Sands Casino, and eventually I earned a rare and precious invite to the Brewing Company, his little alpine oasis, and in one of those strange and beautiful Faulknerian twists that life affords us, I once had a protracted street-fight with Gailmarie's deranged ex-husband. And Don married her. It worked out well for everyone.

As luck would have it, Don was headed to the Brewing Company himself (married men almost always move to town) to salvage some firewood, to putter around the cabin and shore it up for winter. And it is a special kind of puttering, I think, when you can look at a building and draw a memory from every nail, every hinge—knowing those secret things that didn't turn out exactly right, something out of square, or out of level, those small faults that no one else will ever see, or even suspect.

And isn't that our lives? Those small defects we harbor about ourselves, knowing they are wrong, but finding some way to live with them anyway?

Next day, I drove out of Santa Barbara County fast, like a movie fugitive escaping a bank heist. I barreled through the desert and on through Bishop, ignoring the thought of relatives I might have visited, performed a locked-wheel skid at the store in Bridgeport to buy a fork (I'd forgotten my high-speed titanium spork), then highballed out of town again until I made the Brewery turnoff, where at last I slowed it down to a crawl, turned up the road and into the trees and the freshest air, where there is no power and cell phones are delightfully useless.

Don was already there, down from Reno, precisely puttering, an amusing spectacle when performed by older men comfortable with solitude, perhaps even an art form. He was wandering around the front porch staring at things, a chair, a length of chain, hands in his pockets. He would take two steps to the right, kick at the skein of snow on the porch, then stare at something else. This went on for a while as I watched. When he was finished we made our greetings warmly. Old friends can do that, no matter how many years it has been, and as I stored my pack and sorted through my gear, Don fired up the hydro-generator he'd built over the creek.

The Brewery came to life then, a few dim lights punching a hole in the early mountain dusk. We made rice and beans, heated tortillas, and sat at the crude window table while a small fire snapped in the stove and the cabin warmed up fast. We talked, filling in the gaps since we'd last met, hauling out laughs and memories of the old regime. After a cold beer, the night coming on and the thread of conversation fraying, I went to bed, pulled a book down from the shelf, and fell asleep with my headlamp on, reading Edward Abbey, and exactly this: "You can't study the darkness by flooding it with light."

The Sweetwater Brewing Company—a name that has nothing to do with craft beer, resonating instead on a higher plane—sits at the steep end of a long, narrow, and lush alpine valley, heavy-snow country whose melt-off feeds a perennial creek. The creek carves a circuitous route down through stands of aspen and pine, through broad swaths of lush grass and willow, ideal grazing country, where sheepherders once summered their flocks before the government kicked them out. A remnant of those days remains in the carvings left by lonely shepherds in the bark of the trees, a gentle reminder that no matter where you may travel upon this planet, no matter how remote or difficult to reach, someone desperately horny was there before you.

The Perverted Forest is a kind of living history museum, names and dates, sexually explicit carvings of varying graphic complexity, an astonishing, funny, and occasionally frightening, journey through the mind of the mountain shepherd.

After breakfast, Don and I walked through the Perverted Forest, and then down through the valley. He was mad at the bear hunters who had discovered his mountain paradise and taken to running their dogs there, trespassing, scaring off wildlife: a confrontational and arrogant lot of flatlanders and yahoos, aliens in outsized pickups and colossal egos. I couldn't help but think, given the right set of circumstances, that it wasn't impossible to disappear a jackass bear hunter in all that wilderness. But this day there were no fresh signs of them, so we turned back up the valley with that small victory in hand.

And anyway, it was time to shoulder my pack. It was time to climb.

It is no small endeavor to race from sea level to the mountains, throw on a heavy pack, and start climbing without a minute of real preparation or training—it's probably stupid, in fact—but purpose is a powerful engine. I had studied the topos, conferred with Don, an accomplished mountaineer, and set my sights on a peak in the ten-thousand-foot range above the valley. The map is never the territory, of course, so I wasn't under any illusions about the challenge. I expected, and wanted, a brutal climb as the necessary price of admission. And it was, in all respects, a brutal climb. Where the road ended beyond the Brewery I fought through a manzanita forest, rimrocked myself twice on steep ledges, and finally, without a better line up the mountain, was forced to sidehill a ridiculous pitch of endless and dangerously loose scree—one step up, three sliding steps down.

You know how this ends. I worked, struggled, and fought my way to the top, the way we must when the payoff is so sharply calculated, and made my camp where the trees ended in boulders and deep snow. It was the top of the mountain, and I could go no further. It was getting dark too, fast, so I built a small fire, stacking rocks to reflect the heat, gathered what wood there was, and fired up my stove for tea. The wind, when it came in relentless gusts, was cold and stark, carrying in it the raw and haunting music of history, something of the age of the earth, the way that crashing waves on an abandoned beach can reach inside of you and suddenly, for a moment, the world is peeled back to its beginnings.

I drank my tea, warming my hands on the canteen, and sat by the small and sawing fire as the sun dropped hard into the far peaks and the light withdrew, snaking like fire through the roiling clouds and back through the canyons until it was gone, and I was most certainly, incredibly, alone to study the darkness.

There was no sleep, of course.

At that altitude, and at that time of year, in a raw camp, even the best sleeping bags aren't enough. I tended the fire and listened to the wind in the rocks and the bristlecone, and I thought about those giants and superheroes, now lost, who had informed my life and perspectives. I thought long and hard about our son, what he might have been. I thought about my wife, and our life together in the foreign country of southern California. I thought about all those things even as I knew that conclusions are difficult to draw—the modern fantasy of closure at best illusory, at worst not even desirable. A hard cold, the kind of cold that defies negotiation, settled in on my camp as I kept feeding the little fire and sparks burned through my jacket, and I shivered against it, mere steps from an actual physical misery, and exactly where I wanted to be. And the night wore on that way, relentless.

I can't tell you any more about it, as much as I would like to. Don't hold that against me. It's a simple story, really: *I went to the woods to live deliberately*. But the essence of any vision, it seems, is what it means to the seer, like a dream, and whatever lessons I took away from that mountain can only be mine.

I was done when I had stayed as long as it took, which is its own kind of satisfaction, and I was better for it. It was time to move on. And so, stiff with the cold, I packed my gear and started into the long descent, for the warmth and welcome of the Brewery, where Don was waiting for me, still puttering, or stacking firewood, or just staring out the window over a cup of coffee, taking in the long sweep of the valley in fall, making sense of his own hard-earned visions in the wilderness.

For the River, with Gratitude

In November, which kicks off the season of giving thanks for the people, places, and things that populate our lives, I received a gift that is likely to stay with me until I am carried off to Happy Acres. And it couldn't have come at a better time, given that sincere little voice in my head that keeps telling me I'm not getting enough done, and that sand is always running through the hourglass.

This gift—a steelhead trip down the lower Deschutes River with the veterans non-profit Warfighter Outfitters—changed something in me. There are a couple of reasons for that, not least of which is a growing concern about what we are doing to the planet all around us.

But above all—and I think it was the river itself that did it—something vital, something intensely human and personal, was revived in me that careers in the Marine Corps and law enforcement had nearly killed.

I've known that vital thing was dying, and I have struggled mightily—drinking far too much, living in a kind of lubricated haze, and diving breathlessly into the murkier regions of my mind—to keep it on life support for a long time. What was revived, brought suddenly and brilliantly back to life, was a profound and deeply held appreciation for the many good things life still brings us.

I am not a great fisherman. I only learned to fly-fish five or six years ago, and am self-taught. I gravitated toward fly-fishing, I think, because it seemed to represent something singularly healthy, something without artifice, and precisely in opposition to the filthy, heart-crushing, and mendacious meat-grinders of foreign deployments and southern California law enforcement.

I saw fly-fishing as an antidote to all of that, and as I learned something about the art, I also noticed and welcomed the sense of pure and focused joy that comes with a thorough immersion in the things of life, rather than the things of despair—which is where I had been living for so long.

At any rate, that's my fly-fishing curriculum vitae, thin as it is. Outside of a magnificent drift trip down the McKenzie River with my good friend Ed Olsen and neighbor Steve Erickson, a full-time guide for the Fly Fisher's Place in Sisters, Oregon, my fishing has been hit or miss and never more than occasional.

Which brings me 'round to our jet-sled trip. This descent into the otherworldly canyons of the lower Deschutes was, I think I can say without overstatement, like being a struggling minor league ballplayer suddenly called up to play for the New York Yankees. That's what it was like for me, anyway, as Brett Miller, founder of Warfighter Outfitters, guided us downriver on a sharp, winter-bright early morning from the boat launch at Mac's.

Brett and I were joined by Jeremiah Spradling, a full-time fly-fishing guide from Farmington, New Mexico, and all of us were dressed against the cold as we jounced downriver over broad riffles and skated around islands choked with cottonwood, sledding in and out of the cold morning shadows—always conscious of the immense walls of the canyon, and the early promise of a bluebird sky.

This was my first time using a spey-casting rig. Brett and Jeremiah, both of them accomplished spey-casters, gave me some pointers and sent me off downriver to develop a feel for the rod, and to learn my place in the purling waters.

There is a necessary rhythm to fly-fishing, I think, at least to do it well. There is some conscious sense of conducting a large orchestra, of knowing when to bring the right instruments up, or tamp them down, or bring them all together, and there were times when I managed a decent cast and could feel the music starting to play. And then I would forget some element of the tune and wrap my line around a willow branch behind my head, or send out a tangled pile of leader and tippet in a ridiculous caricature of grace.

But I didn't care. What I felt, standing bellybutton deep in the dark rushing water—watched by herds of bighorn sheep in the canyon walls above, or by a bald eagle on a tree branch on the other side of the river—was pure exhilaration and appreciation that we have these waters at all; that they are still clean enough to support populations of steelhead, who have been making their spawning runs here since sabre-toothed tigers and woolly mammoths roamed the valleys of Los Angeles.

It's possible too, I think, to get so lost in the act of fly-fishing that it is a kind of baptism, so that coming out of the river is a spiritual rebirth. I think that because that is exactly what happened to me. We traveled miles downriver, stopping here and there to anchor the boat in the rocks or around a tree, and wade into the waters to fish, or simply to watch the bighorns, or the birds, or to listen to the water rippling over stones in the shallows and lapping in cold eddies along a cutbank. All of that, the quiet dimensions of it, reached deep into the recesses of my mind, and then turned it inside-out.

Jumping out of the boat at the end of the day I felt, for the first time in many years, that my long struggles with the depressions and darker turns of mind—caused by the soul-sucking rigors and realities of duty—were finally, in a meaningful way, cut loose.

I can't totally explain it. But I know that without the river, without that canyon lifted from the Pleistocene, without that day full of wading and slipping on rocks, of swinging a prayer into the cold, silvery waters, it would not have happened. Not the way it did. It was as if all the troubles I have been trying to shake were rinsed clean, becoming something I can examine and turn over in my hands like a museum piece, rather than feel coursing through my bloodstream each day like a warm shot of poison.

At the end of the day, without catching a fish or even feeling a bite, I felt twenty years younger in my soul.

Gifts like that can save a life. That day we had mile upon mile of the river completely to ourselves. And now, as I think about it, I suppose we always have the river completely to ourselves, even when—perhaps especially when—we appreciate, and seek to share the gifts that it has given us.

Sinatra at Ground Zero

Our American obsession with celebrity is as interesting as it is potentially dangerous. It's also hard to dislodge, as war correspondent George Weller discovered when he defied McArthur's ban on travel to Nagasaki after the Army Air Corps detonated Fat Man, a twenty-one-kiloton nuclear weapon, over the city.

Nearly a thousand allied POWs were living in Nagasaki, interned as slave labor in the Mitsubishi war plants. Most of them were starving to death, or being beaten to death, or suffering from curable diseases for which the Japanese—who routinely looted Red Cross packages meant for the prisoners—withheld even basic medicines.

And if it was possible to make their tortured lives any worse, on August 9, 1945, they were also living at ground zero.

Seven Dutch and one British prisoner died instantly when the bomb detonated at approximately fifteen hundred feet over the city, a blast of such magnitude that it seared the shadows of trees and human beings into concrete. Most of the surviving prisoners were just plain lucky, but many of them had also had the foresight, after the Hiroshima bombing—which they witnessed from their prison camps in Nagasaki—to realize the existence of some new weapon of unimaginable ferocity, and had dug what trenches they could for shelter against a similar event.

Weller, encountering some of these survivors when he slipped into the city following the formal Japanese surrender, also encountered our American celebrity obsession in an interesting way.

Interviewing Australians, he found they were mostly interested in which horse had won the Melbourne Cup. British prisoners wanted to know if Churchill was still prime minister, or if the government had gone over to Labour. The Dutch POWs wanted to know if Princess Juliana's third child was a male heir to the throne.

But the Americans, likewise starving, brutalized, and now nuked, had more pressing concerns. One of them said, "B-29s dropping us food keep enclosing Saipan newspapers with stuff about some guy named Sinatra. Who is he and what's his racket?"

That kind of abiding interest in mere celebrity hasn't waned much. One might even argue that in its ultimate expression—and celebrity worship has certainly been refined over the years—it handed Donald Trump the keys to the White House. Worse—and proof that we truly are a stubborn and slow-learning lot—it appears poised to do it again, should the very stable genius pass the orb and sceptre off to Oprah Winfrey.

Who knows if she'll actually run, but as a policy it's probably better to avoid drawing too much political inspiration from the well of celebrity narcissists.

There are probably sound reasons to avoid leaning on celebrities for much of anything at all, actually. It would seem prudent, at least to avoid falling down a psychiatric rabbit hole, to exercise extreme caution before mimicking the opinions of people who spend most of their time pretending to be somebody else.

Of course, being really good at pretending to be somebody else is also incredibly lucrative, and having a lot of money is still too often confused with the possession of excellent opinions about how better to inhabit the planet.

Sean Penn, for instance, still believes the Chavez revolution was a great move for Venezuela, never mind the resulting starvation, food riots, government-sanctioned murder of political opposition, the collapse of even basic government services, or one million percent inflation. *Chavismo!*

Exercises in self-adoration such as the Golden Globes, or that nauseating exhibition of preening called the Oscars—where no award-winner would miss a chance to re-educate a rapt global audience—probably help to cement the popular misunderstanding that celebrity, all by itself, lends gravitas to whatever it is that celebrities say.

It doesn't, and sometimes even the most carefully managed and strategically marketed public persona develops a revealing crack.

Winfrey's otherwise appropriate excoriation of sexual harassment, for example, would be a lot more convincing without the embarrassing pictures of her fawning over Harvey Weinstein at cocktail parties; and her opinions on racial relations would ring truer absent her suggestion to the BBC that generations of older people—one suspects she meant mostly white people—will need to hurry up and die in order to usher in the golden age of racial harmony.

Probably the most annoying part of these spectacles is the endless parade of narcissism—which often rivals Trump's in its insistence on celebrity as the natural birthplace of wisdom.

At any rate, back in Nagasaki, those starving and scarred POWs who endured years of terror at the hands of sadists, and who somehow even survived a nuclear thumping delivered by their own countrymen, were at least clever enough to suspect that Sinatra was part of some kind of celebrity racket.

They were smart enough to see it even if—after everything they had learned about the darker heart of human nature—they couldn't wait to get back home, eat a real meal, and dance those horrors away to the sound of his voice.

The Digital Dictatorship

Nobody seems to know, from sea to shining sea, what is wrong with our fair Republic.

Added to the palpable environments of disorientation, we are witnessing widespread outbursts of anger and frustration—and not just in the US, but from London to Paris, from Berlin to Brussels. This is true while at the same time the traditional sources of authority and leadership—from the U.S. Congress to the House of Commons—don't seem to have any answers.

It's quite clear at this point, under the spell of this worldwide fin de siècle funk, that we are on the precipice of falling into a profoundly different world—a fact which is deeply unsettling to hundreds of millions of people—even if they can't quite articulate precisely what it is that bothers them.

A couple of weeks ago I wrote a column piece called "The Great American Freak Out" for the newspaper. In the piece I toyed with an idea that has been floating around in my head for a while—the relatively new phenomenon of American adults losing their marbles in sudden and spectacular failures of self-discipline. I wrote: "If the now-ubiquitous American Freak Out is evidence of anything, perhaps it is a symptom of our lives on the new frontier. Maybe it's happening because we are culturally marooned, neither here nor there just yet, but rather groaning through the death agonies of the old myths that once sustained us, while fighting savagely over the invention and control of the new myths we will eventually live by."

I was thinking of human beings as free-agents when I wrote that, and I think there is some truth in it, but what I wasn't considering was the notion that our 18th century ideas about free-will, and human free-agency, are increasingly inadequate to address the realities of 21st century life on earth. What I think I've discovered since writing that piece is that many of the people who are involved in these freak-out dramas have been hacked. They are no longer free-agents. They actually have no recognizable free-will whatsoever. They are bio-technical zombies.

So it was serendipitous when I cracked Yuval Noah Harari's latest masterpiece, *21 Lessons for the 21st Century*. Harari's principle effort is to force us to pay attention to what is happening *today*, and to come to our own conclusions about whether the relentless mining of the past is going to work anymore to build a reliable trail into the future.

Harari believes, and I think correctly, that we are now experiencing a kind of industrial revolution that is so revolutionary, so game-changing, that our traditional philosophical underpinnings and the institutions they created are woefully unprepared to address what is happening. Furthermore, Harari stresses that the individual who doesn't understand the power of Artificial Intelligence at work in our culture cannot possibly understand what it is that we are looking at, right now, directly in front of us. And if we can't see the forest for the trees, how can we expect to make intelligent decisions going forward?

A recent string of Congressional hearings—where various Big Data bigshots like Mark Zuckerburg have been hauled in on the carpet to account for data breaches—are most revealing because of the questions that *aren't* being asked. And those questions aren't being asked because Congress, and most every average American, has no real grasp on the power that algorithms and AI are asserting over the daily living and the direction of modern life. Harari argues that the reason we aren't asking the right questions is that we are now in the uncomfortable arena created by philosophical impoverishment. The questions we have always asked, and the institutions we have looked to for answers, are no longer sufficient to the task of providing answers in a world whose decision-making loops are increasingly dominated by Big Data and AI algorithms.

Harari makes extremely powerful and compelling arguments in defense of his thesis, beginning with an explanation of what AI is, versus what it isn't, who is using it, and how it is being used to capture and hold the attention of billions of people on earth—and then to influence their thinking by subtle suggestion.

Most importantly, Harari wants his readers to understand that our ideas about free-will, and human agency, are under bombardment. Harari argues, and I think convincingly, that the human mind is not sacrosanct and inviolable. Not anymore. The sad fact is that in the 21st century the human mind can be hacked, and it is in fact now being hacked on a pervasive scale.

Tristan Harris, a former "design ethicist" at Google, and founder of Humanetech—who together with Harari is on the forefront of trying to wake the world up to the forces that are helping to create the widespread disorientation and disillusionment in our culture, told The Wire that by using big data algorithms and supercomputers directed at each and every user, "You can precisely target a lie directly to the people who are most susceptible."

This is undeniably so, and by orders of magnitude. What concerns Harris and Harari, and should probably be of great concern to all of us, are the effects of invisible supercomputers pointed directly at each and every one of us, and then again on the downstream effects that will unavoidably have on the liberal underpinnings of Western civilization. If you live downstream from DuPont, don't wake up surprised when you have cancer caused by the Teflon chemicals coursing through your veins. Western liberalism has thus far proven remarkably elastic in the face of enormous political and economic challenges, but Harari and Harris argue that this newest test may be the most formidable of all. And, worse yet, they are not convinced it will survive.

Harari:

> *"Democracy assumes that human feelings reflect a mysterious and profound 'free will,' that this 'free will' is the ultimate source of authority, and that while some people are more intelligent than others, all humans are equally free. Like Einstein and Dawkins, an illiterate maid also has free will, and therefore on election-day her feelings—represented by her vote—count just as much as anybody else's. ... This reliance on the heart might prove to be the Achilles' heel of liberal democracy. For once somebody (whether in Beijing or in San Francisco) gains the technological ability to hack and manipulate the human heart, democratic politics will mutate into an emotional puppet show."*

It would be hard to argue that this isn't already the case, as the recent "Smirking Boy" incident in front of the Lincoln Memorial, in which a group of Black Nationalist crazies, a busload of smarmy Catholic school boys, and a handful of Native American activists kicked off one of the larger and more ridiculous emoti-political media shitstorms in recent memory. And much of that cyclone of stupidity was driven by AI—supercomputers, design engineers, and control rooms—aware of and responding to the emotional and political preferences of two billion Facebook accounts, and countless hundreds of millions of newsfeeds and Snapchats and Instagram clients.

The Smirking Boy incident created its own weather system and then rained garbage on the entire world for days.

This episode also pulls back the curtain on the pervasive lie: that social media and other networks were meant to create interactive communities across the spectrum, and would draw people into conversations that expanded the mind and our ability to connect on the human plane. To an extraordinary degree, the opposite is true. Social and other forms of media, having hacked millions of minds, now carry their users off on strong digital currents, eventually depositing them on islands of ignorance and loneliness. News outlets, which were once a defense against ignorance, now serve only help to stoke the fires and perpetuate the problems. So much so that the consumer ends up like a marooned man walking endlessly around the same island, seeing the same palm tree, the same forlorn beach, the same vast ocean, the same skulking seagulls. According to Harris, "70% of 1.9 billion users of YouTube are watching videos chosen [for them] by an algorithm. That's more people than follow Islam."

Under these conditions, the ability to converse and exchange thoughts in a face-to-face marketplace appears to be a thing of the past. Under these isolated conditions and in these engineered environments, it's no wonder that children can't talk to their parents, parents can't talk to their children, students can't talk to teachers, teachers can't talk to students, parents can't talk to teachers, teachers can't talk to parents, neighbors never talk to each other at all, nobody can talk to the cops, and Congress is incapable of listening. Even television news panels, stacked with powdered wigs and big brains, devolve into shouting matches, so much so that a disinterested observer can't even understand what they are saying.

We have trouble talking to each other because so many people have been sucked away on the algorithms meant to charge the dopamine response in their brains, and they are almost incapable of entertaining information that comes from outside of the bubble that AI has created for them based on their own preferences. The effects of digital isolation are so bad that an entire industry now exists merely to re-teach human beings how to sit down in the same room and have a conversation.

This is a real thing that is happening right now. Every day.

Harari backstops the thought:

> *"Soon authority might shift again—from humans to algorithms ... Just as divine authority was legitimized by religious mythologies, and human authority was justified by the liberal story, so the coming technological revolution might establish the authority of Big Data algorithms, while undermining the very idea of individual freedom."*

Because the real game in modern life is data. Who has it, and who controls it. How do we live in a future where human doctors are eventually replaced by AI doctors—because AI doctors are extremely inexpensive, don't require 10 years of schooling, and make fewer diagnostic mistakes. What happens when insurance companies refuse to insure anyone who does not sign up for an AI doctor? Or when they refuse to insure a driver who won't buy a self-driving car, given that networked autonomous vehicles will have far fewer accidents. How do workers unite to protect themselves in mushroom industries that bloom for ten years and disappear? How does one even live without surrendering one's own data to unaccountable Big Data corporations who buy and sell information about people? Who regulates this? Who is accountable? Where is Congress? Does individual agency matter anymore in an AI world where integrated supercomputers collate data faster and better than human beings, and where policy makers increasingly rely on them for economic theory or political platforms?

It's tempting to just spit out a wad of tobacco and utter an ironic pshaw, but ignoring these questions isn't going to make them go away.

This is the world that is being created all around us, at increasing speed, every day. And it's leaving a lot of what we thought we knew about life in the dust.

Harari:

> *"In ancient times land was the most important asset in the world, politics was a struggle to control land, and if too much land became concentrated in too few hands, society split into aristocrats and commoners. In the modern era machines and factories became more important than land, and political struggles focused on controlling these vital means of production. If too many of the machines became concentrated in too few hands, society split into capitalists and proletarians. In the twenty first century, however, data will eclipse both land and machinery as the most important asset, and politics will be a struggle to control the flow of data. If data becomes concentrated in too few hands, humankind will split into different species.*
>
> *"The race to obtain the data is already on, headed by data giants such as Google, Facebook, Baidu, and Tencent. So far, many of these giants seem to have adopted the business model of 'attention merchants.' They capture our attention by providing us with free information, services, and entertainment, and they then resell our attention to advertisers. Yet the data giants probably aim far higher than any previous attention merchant. Their true business isn't to sell advertisements at all. Rather, by capturing our attention they manage to accumulate immense amounts of data about us, which is worth more than any advertising revenue. We aren't their customers—we are their product."*

The truth is startling. What's more startling is that from a very young age Americans and other children around the world are being sucked into the data pool, whether they know it or not, and whether or not it is any good for them. And nobody seems to know how to stop the machine long enough to get off.

Harari:

> *"Ordinary humans will find it very difficult to resist this process. At present, people are happy to give away their most valuable asset—their personal data—in exchange for free email services and funny cat videos. It's a bit like African and Native American tribes who unwittingly sold entire countries to European imperialists in exchange for colorful beads and cheap trinkets. If, later on, ordinary people decide to try to block the flow of data, they might find it increasingly difficult, especially as they might come to rely on the network for all their decisions, and even for their healthcare and physical survival."*

This world is already much closer to the new reality than we think, which exists in its identifiable infant stages—the ongoing hubbub about Russian use of social media during the last election, fear of "deepfakes," bots and memes, and the buying and selling of data collections by large corporations. And it's clear that the early stages of this paradigm shift underwrite a great deal of the confusion and desperation we are seeing all around us. Harari writes: "In 1938 humans were offered three global stories to choose from, in 1968 just two, and in 1998 a single story seemed to prevail. In 2018 we are down to zero. No wonder that the liberal elites, who dominated much of the world in recent decades, are in a state of shock and disorientation. ... To be suddenly left without any story is terrifying. Nothing makes any sense."

And by "liberal elites," Harari is not talking about leftist professors in the LaLa Empires of university campuses—he's talking about all of us in the Western digital world.

We can begin to make sense of the confusion if we become more aware of what this newest industrial revolution portends—how it effects us individually—and begin to shape our lives with the full knowledge of its potential for harm. We should also be aware of its potential for good. Because that exists also. Either way, there are going to be unavoidable, and massive effects, and we are beginning to see those too. Ask any high school teacher about the effects of the digital world on the attention span of their students. My personal concern is how to minimize becoming part of the unforeseen collateral damage—to avoid becoming one with the bomb crater.

We have long heard stories that AI will eventually push people out of the workforce. This is true, and will likely make many humans suddenly irrelevant. Harari suggests that it will not only make many humans irrelevant in the workplace, but that on a worldwide scale it may also eventually create a near-permanent "useless class," that is, people completely unable to participate in a ubiquitously AI workplace. Whereas in the past an unemployed farmer might take a job in a factory, by "... 2050 a cashier or textile worker losing her job to a robot will not be able to start working as a cancer researcher, as a drone operator, or as part of a human-AI banking team. She won't have the necessary skills."

The pervasiveness of AI may in fact deprive the world of many of its "fall-back" employment options. Imagine the effect of billions of unemployed, and unemployable, people.

Harari:

> *"Not only does AI stand poised to hack humans and outperform them in what were hitherto uniquely human skills, but it also enjoys uniquely nonhuman abilities, which make the difference between AI and a human worker one of a kind rather than merely of degree. Two particularly important nonhuman abilities that AI possesses are connectivity and updatability. ... What we are facing is not the replacement of millions of individual human workers by millions of individual robots and computers; rather, individual humans are likely to be replaced by an integrated network. ... Notwithstanding the danger of mass unemployment, what we should worry about even more is the shift in authority from humans to algorithms, which might destroy any remaining faith in the liberal story and open the way to the rise of digital dictatorships. ... Once AI makes better decisions than we do about careers*

and perhaps even relationships, our concept of humanity and of life will have to change. Humans are used to thinking about life as a drama of decision-making. Liberal democracy and free-market capitalism see the individual as an autonomous agent constantly making choices about the world. ... What will happen to this view of life as we increasingly rely on AI to make decisions for us? At present we trust Netflix to recommend movies, and Google Maps to choose whether we turn right or left. But once we begin to count on AI to decide what to study, where to work, and whom to marry, human life will cease to be a drama of decision-making. Democratic elections and free markets will make little sense. ... Democracy in its present form cannot survive the merger of biotech and infotech. Either democracy will successfully reinvent itself in a radically new form or humans will come to live in 'digital dictatorships.'"

He goes on to point out that these new dictatorships will look entirely different than anything we have seen thus far. They will "be as different from Nazi Germany as Nazi Germany was different from Ancien Régime France."

So this is our challenge. We are fortunate the big minds like Harari and Harris are scouting the landscape out in front of us, and returning to the campfire with advice on how to navigate its perils. Because the power of AI resides in its ability to infect us in the same way that smallpox blankets infected Native Americans. It's largely invisible, and in the moment it may even feel like a good way to stay warm in the winter. But this kind of trade is very dangerous, and if we aren't careful it may even prove to be fatal.

Stealing Signs

One August, my wife and I turned the ranch chores over to a hungry University of Oregon student, packed up the dogs, extra water and a chainsaw, and blasted southeast out of the trees onto the basalt and granite outback country of southeastern Oregon. Through Silver Lake then, home of that marvelous dining mystery known as the Cowboy Dinner Tree, and on through the beautiful, lazy curves of Summer Lake and the Paisley Caves where—God bless them—scientists have discovered the oldest fossilized North American human turds, known as *coprolites*.

We stopped for lunch in the tiny desert hamlet of Paisley, headquarters of the mighty ZX Ranch. Chicken-fried steak and eggs (hold the gravy), Merle Haggard singing about his mother, and prison, on the counter radio. Then we jumped back in the truck and headed south again through Valley Falls where great herds of pronghorn were moving through the buckbrush and alfalfa.

Much of the drive was a highway chess-match with slipshod caravans of "Burners" on their way south to the Black Rock Desert and Burning Man, who jammed the narrow highway with every conceivable type of contraption, including one old man at the helm of what appeared to be a fully operational steam-calliope. Still, not even a heavy migration of Burners can entirely wreck the view of southeastern Oregon with baseball playing on the radio and the sun shining on the farthest buttes. So we drove on, through Lakeview, and finally over Cedar Pass into the Great Basin and Cedarville, California.

I must confess now—and for all time—my intention to commit a couple of felonies on this trip. It was not the primary motivation for our sojourn; it would come down more as a crime of opportunity, but I did, in fact, leave the ranch fully intending, and with malice aforethought, to steal a road sign.

The plan was to break out my trusty Stihl chainsaw on the side of a dark road, saw through the post, stash the loot under a blanket, and transport it back across state lines, thereby becoming a full-fledged Enemy of the State. My wife was to serve as lookout and getaway driver, wrapping her firmly into the conspiracy, and exposing us both to the potential of that particularly embarrassing modern phenomenon: *the viral internet mugshot.* Still, we felt pretty good about the operation.

It is a great American tradition to decorate barns with road signs, and our barn walls are decidedly naked, in need of upgrade, and we were, after all, in pursuit of a rare and distinctive prize: a Nevada-style "Open Range" sign.

To the highway-sign connoisseur, the Nevada version of the open-range totem is an artistic gem: a rare and distinctive illustration of an actual wild cow, on the fight, afraid of nothing, daring you to strike it. It is a road sign with panache, a rare moment of government inspiration, and far superior to the California or Oregon versions, which feature a domesticated, melancholy, cud-munching dairy cow.

But first, the Cedarville Fair. A quick word about the Cedarville Fair: if you are casting about in our post-modern, save-the-snowy-plover, ban-fracking universe for a cause, try doing something—anything—to save the Cedarville Fair which, like the life it reflects at every turn, is in danger of disappearing under the flood of global nonsense. Grab a room at Surprise Valley Hot Springs (avoid #2, or #15) then drive into town. Getting into the fair will cost you three bucks at the gate, and once inside you'll be surrounded by suntanned ranch kids in cowboy hats, young girls loping their horses simply everywhere, working sheep-dog trials, a greased-pig contest, and worn-out buckaroos, seemingly carved out of juniper, asleep in the shade of the cottonwoods. And try the Basque barbecue on Thursday night: lamb chops and homemade bread, a plop of salad, a plastic cup full of red wine, a picnic table all your own, and The Heartless Band tuning up on stage. Alas, you could do much worse in a bid to save something on the planet.

Friday morning was the horseshow, where we watched my dear old mum pick up a blue ribbon—cheers for the old girl—and afterward we all headed in for lunch at The Country Hearth, already overflowing with Burners in search of a final decent meal before the Black Rock playa and that alternative universe. The service was sporadic but the food was good, and after goodbyes, Wendy and I drove south, down through Eagleville, across the state line into Nevada, where once upon a time I lived in a shack on the edge of Duck Lake—dry since about the time those Paisley turds were laid down—and wondered often in the pages of my daybook where I might be, and what my life might look like, twenty years forth.

Well, old self, it turns out if you ride a circle long enough, say twenty years, you might end up where you started, and one day crest a hill amused to see your old camp still sitting there, still forlorn in that vast Nevada emptiness, a gunmetal shack in the occasional shade of a homesteader's plot of Lombardy poplars.

They'd improved the place some, and gone to haying. The old horse corrals were still there, but there was an industrial scale to the pole barns and pivot irrigation that simply didn't exist when I lived there. We couldn't get through the gate, now adorned with an outright lie warning copper thieves of monitored video surveillance, but I wouldn't have pushed through anyway. All I wanted to do—all I needed to do—was blow a kiss in that direction.

Instead, we turned back onto the Wall Canyon Road, jouncing over rocks, fording dry streambeds, pushing deeper into the desert where I once rode the ridgelines looking for stray cattle, singing out loud to myself, scaring my horse and the wildlife. Were we still hunting for a road sign, then? I doubt it. I was showing off to my wife, resurrecting ghosts of an old life, chasing memories up out of the brush and the rocks and the deep-cut canyons. Mostly, we filled the truck with powdery dust.

Back to the highway then, the sun setting, driving north, we dodged the southbound parade of high speed Burners tearing up the road, and made it back to our room before sunset. We poured out some cowboy coolers (boxed wine, ice, and 7UP), then took a long and satisfying soak in the mildly sulfurous tub. We read books. We took the dogs out for a final piss in the rabbitbrush. And we slept like royalty, I think, even on a bad mattress, even with the windows open to a cold night breeze and the yip of coyotes in the dark, our minds tired and open to suggestion, desert views playing out in our dreams.

And the desert, when you see it right, can envelop you like that, can't it, and hold you like a lover, stroking your forehead and telling a good story to help you sleep.

In the morning, out of food, we charged out east, feasting on Peanut M&M's and a handful of jerky, blowing over a cattle guard where the California asphalt gave way to Nevada and the blessing of dirt roads, following the corduroy trails into the sheer cant of sunrise in August, where the light plays tricks in the rocks and the sage, stretching basin into range, range into basin, and every crested hill reveals another deceptive view to the far horizon.

We drove this way for hours, feeling the first hint of fall in the crisp wind rushing out of the canyons, until we made it to Steven's Camp, near the north gate of High Rock Canyon and the Applegate Trail, where dreams once perished in starvation, madness, and Indian attacks.

I wondered then, in the middle of that hard nowhere, staring out across the High Rock country, what one of those pioneers would think of the modern Burners, and just how much those seventy thousand Burners who assemble for their party on the playa actually know about the Black Rock Desert.

Have they read the stories, or heard the tales, of oxen stampeding for water only to scald and die in the double-hot pools on the western edge of the playa? Do they know about a certain young girl, dying of thirst, who got into her mother's bottle of laudanum and died there, overdosed on the playa while her mother wailed against a sky the color of iron, and the men, now skin and bones, dug into that hardpan with spoons to bury her?

Perhaps they do. And maybe it simply doesn't matter if they do, or if they don't.

We let the dogs run and explored Steven's Camp, where someone had recently killed a deer and skinned it under the hanging pole, leaving only a gut pile, a ribcage and a pair of hooves. We stood listening to the wind in the rocks, the water running through cattails and deep green grass, until the call of the road, and our own home, couldn't be ignored.

We never did get our sign, Nevada having adopted yet another tragic California habit of mindless conformity.

So, instead of adorning our criminal records with a marvelous felony, we settled for a country fair, for a chance to see my mother enjoying her life, for scattered memories in that unreal desert—*ever may it be so*—of abandoned cow camps in the dry basins, massive mule deer bucks in the sage, the quick artesian springs at Steven's Camp, and the ghost of a young girl from a thousand years ago.

There were the Burners too, a kind of modern pioneer, I suppose, broken down on the side of the road, their possibles scattered in a search for just the right tool, their clothes ruined, their hair in dreads, determined to finish the trail. But we drove home happier for all of that, against the traffic, still blameless in the eyes of the law, the dogs exhausted, and back toward home through a big and beautiful emptiness with the magic of Saturday baseball beamed into us via satellite radio. We covered those empty miles listening to the Yankees and White Sox three thousand miles away, where it was Joe Torre day in the Bronx, and the batter was busy reading the seams on a circle change-up with two on and one out, the base runners peering in against the glare, watching the catcher, stealing signs of their own.

Breakfast on the Blue Nile

My wife and I like to eat out. We don't think of ourselves as, say, Truman Capote and Joanne Carson dining at La Cote Basque, but we do enjoy the occasional easy weekend brunch in Sisters town, where we often bump into people we know and value, and spend a few pleasant minutes catching up.

And really, that's all we had in mind a few days ago when we were seated, handed our menus, and ordered up some coffee at our favorite breakfast joint.

Sometimes such an easy thing just isn't meant to be.

No sooner had we been seated than a woman, unknown to us, and sitting with a companion across the otherwise empty room, launched into a forcefully loud and seemingly endless political tirade.

It quickly became clear that she was not directing the diatribe directly at her companion, or even directly at us, necessarily, but she clearly felt compelled to speak loudly enough, and belligerently enough, to be heard by everyone.

Because, after a time, I had noticed her referencing our table after each new cast of political virtue—as if watching a bobber on the lake—I couldn't help but think that she might have been triggered by my cowboy hat.

To a certain turn of mind, the cowboy hat is a notorious symbol of overwrought and ultimately dull, machismo. To these folks the cowboy hat represents the historical oppression of otherwise virtuous bank robbers, genocide, and the indefensible subjugation of bovines. Merely seeing a cowboy hat, to some people, can loosen a cascade of repressed emotion. Never mind that some us wear them mostly because, as in my case, we are bald, and prefer the luxury of ample shade over the risks of melanoma.

And maybe it wasn't that at all. Maybe it was just an outbreak of "sudden theater."

Whatever the cause, my wife and I ordered our food and sat looking at each other wistfully across the table while being treated to a somewhat stumpy harangue on the full litany of American evils. It came from a particular side of the political divide, but in matters of bad manners affiliation hardly matters. The invective that spilled forth, while her companion tried valiantly to bring reason—speaking in that lower and slower voice reserved for embarrassed adults in the face of misbehaving children—would have made the saltiest Navy Chief blush.

We had options. I thought, momentarily, of addressing the outraged djinn across the room with a request for self-restraint, this being the cozy mountain town of Sisters, after all, and well before noon, but the cop in me thought better of saying anything at all. One of the first rules of police work is ironclad: never try to reason with a drunk.

Not that she was drunk, she wasn't, but there is another rule in there too, which has more to do with letting someone lean so far into their opinions that they eventually fall over.

Also, sticking it out was more in line with our commitment to an ultimate victory over the purely mundane, a vision of our lives lived less on the spectrum of endlessly repetitive and predictable ritual, and more as a thoroughly wild expedition up the Blue Nile.

Mindset matters, naturally, but more importantly: the food was terrific.

So we endured and pondered the mysteries. My wife and I ate in virtual silence, forced into the role of a captured and unwilling audience, reduced to communicating through a kind of method-acting pantomime that would have thrilled Lee Strasberg, and which every married couple out in the field knows quite well.

What fueled this woman's outrage at the machine, which had obviously been bubbling for some time and which she felt duty bound to share with everyone in the restaurant was, I think now, a kind of rage born of impotence. There was desperation in her vibrato wails against the various agonies of empire, but in the end, though I doubt she could see it, the result was a spectacular demonstration of juvenile pathos rather than a persuasive call to man the barricades.

It occurred to me, as I shoveled a beautifully crafted omelet into my face, that the larger problem wasn't this woman's opinions because, really, who cares? It was her obsession with theater over debate, as she made repeatedly clear during her monologue that opposition to her views, or even moderation of her positions, was an intolerable affront.

It is a common modern failing: the inability to distinguish the difference between highly viewable or highly illuminating, opinions.

I'm tracking a lot more of that sort of thing lately, though there is a sound argument to be made that the root blame belongs to ABC News, who in the 1968 presidential campaign chose to feature debates between Gore Vidal and William F. Buckley rather than the standard "gavel-to-gavel" coverage of the conventions. It was those debates, which famously concluded with Buckley losing his grip and threatening to punch Vidal in the nose, which ushered in the age of televised political punditry from which we may never, it seems now, recover.

For our endurance, the hostess—long suffering herself—gave us a thoughtful certificate for ten-percent off at our next visit. She didn't have to say anything at all, and neither did we, as we passed outside into the strange light and primordial smoke from the seemingly endless forest fires.

And, with the passage of a little time, the whole episode now puts me in the mind of Wallace Stevens, who wrote in *The Snow Man* how important it is for the unwilling audience to hear in these kinds of passionate, theatrical, and sometimes inappropriate outbursts, both the "Nothing that is not there and the nothing that is."

Notes on a Greasy Napkin

I like to write in diners. I like it because I always hear something marvelous about politics, or the weather, and also because there is something inspirational in the smell of bacon, the comfort of a worn-out booth beside a picture window, and the reliable goodness of hashed browns, two eggs over-medium, and a side of English muffins.

One day last week saw me in a booth early enough to enjoy Sisters in that golden hour—you know the one I mean—when the kids are all in school and the shops are just opening up, right before Cascade Avenue is shaken to pieces by eighteen-wheelers jake-braking through the crosswalks.

There were four men at the counter—of Korean War vintage—who were talking about the weather. One of them mentioned the weather in Kentucky, pointing out that it was three degrees in Lexington. The guy in the red ballcap suggested that that was another reason not to live in Kentucky, which was seconded and passed without objection.

I've never been to Kentucky, so I have nothing to add. What I imagine is a triptych of Americana: picture-book thoroughbred farms, distillery smokestacks, and Pentecostals up the holler handling snakes in a clapboard church. There is no reason to believe any of those images are accurate but it's what pops into my head whenever I hear the word "Kentucky."

I let the thought go—I was hitchhiking on the whole conversation anyway, which is a singular pleasure of writing in diners—and focused instead on my breakfast, which came out fast and hot and brilliant.

I generally avoid any eatery with pictures of food on the menu. I understand that many modern customers are visual learners and, this being 21st century America, they probably need a color photo to assist with reading comprehension, but a proper menu should insist on literacy, which is why the only pictures on it should be of western landscapes, horses, or guns.

I always add a dash of Tabasco to my plate. Lately, I've noticed that a lot of diners are pushing green Cholula in the condiments basket, but I never put any kind of green sauce on my food. Particularly breakfast. Red sauce, or no sauce, is my gringo sauce bias.

The sausage patty was thin but seasoned right. This is important because a fry cook who can't season industrial sausage to a certain level of palatability is a sad person. The eggs were slightly under-medium, but this is forgivable if, and only if, the English muffins are hot and slathered properly in butter.

Back at the counter, the red-ballcap guy was talking about the perfect place to build another Bi-Mart, which he thought was probably Hailey, Idaho.

Great diners serve two English muffins. Since one primary purpose of roadside diners is to nurture our generosity, serving up one lukewarm English muffin, or the sad spectacle of diced "country potatoes" in place of traditional hashed browns, will never earn a gold spatula in "Rullman's Guide to Greasy Spoons."

Outside, Sisters was coming to life and the booth next to me suddenly filled up with two businessmen and one laptop. Eavesdropping—"fieldwork" is the preferred term—I gathered they were building a new company and fairly serious about eventual world domination.

That's when the waitress asked the older one if he was wearing socks, which was an awkward opening but seemed to knock their talk of private jets and presidential suites down a peg.

Which is another thing: there is both skill and art to waitressing a diner. That's true of any restaurant, but in an old-school diner the waitress is a stand-up pro and can leave you either titillated or terrified—her choice.

Meanwhile, talk at the counter had run full circle and was back to weather. The red-ballcap guy—who was now fairly wired on caffeine and exaggerating his gestures—brought up George Carlin's "Hippy Dippy Weatherman" routine.

This got my attention.

They flirted with a consensus that the routine was brilliant except, I noticed, green-ballcap guy on the far end was holding out. He stared into his coffee cup until, after long internal deliberation, he looked straight ahead at the pies and then said quietly: "He was whacked out all the time; but yes, he was a very funny man."

I was proud of green-ballcap in that moment. I was proud of him because admitting such a thing in public was obviously an act of personal bravery. It was as if a whistle had suddenly blown and he was now crawling out of a muddy emotional trench and going over the top with a knife in his teeth. Truth is, I'd been rooting for him all through my last savory bites, since he seemed to be tamping down a growing list of differences with red-ballcap.

I have no idea if any of that is true, but that's how my mind wanders in restaurants.

Mostly, I liked all the talk about the weather because it resurrected some of Al Sleet's long overlooked Hippy Dippy wisdom, which in our great new age of angry binary politics still has suction. Sleet admonished us, you may recall, to study the difference between a Canadian Low and a Mexican High, and optimistically suggested that "The weather will continue to change for a long, long time."

The Petrified Man

In 1782 Ben Franklin published a fake edition of an otherwise real newspaper. It was meant to curry sympathy for American resistance to the British by claiming that natives allied with the British were on the warpath, slaughtering settlers by the hundreds. Complete with phony ads and other articles, it was all fake news.

Fake news becomes fake news when it is published, or broadcast, by an otherwise reliable source. Conversely, when fake newspapers publish real news the whole centrifuge is thrown out of balance, so maybe they shouldn't do that, either. But even when real newspapers stick to real news, and fake newspapers stick to publishing fake stories, the results can be confusing.

For instance, it may be impossible to disprove the *Weekly World News'* claims that a redneck vampire attacked a trailer park in Kentucky, that a mermaid cemetery was discovered in the Atlantic, or that a woman in British Columbia was Bigfoot's love slave. In front of a modern jury, which is essentially a collection of licensed drivers, those claims might be much easier to defend than to prosecute as taradiddles.

And in an alarming twist, "real news" headlines are often more difficult to swallow than tabloid fantasies: "Scientists Breed Glow-in-the-Dark Rabbits" we are told—which is both bizarre and true; or this gem from the revered BBC: "Stoned Wallabies Make Crop Circles."

At any rate, we seem to love a good "fake news" villain, and a plank-holder in that realm is—beyond any reasonable doubt—Mark Twain. Twain didn't invent fake news—but he most certainly grasped the possibilities and flogged them with all of the zest and vigor befitting the energies of a Wild West boomtown.

Twain arrived in Virginia City, Nevada Territory, in 1861. After two years of cynical efforts to strike it rich on the Comstock Lode, he fell into newspapering and began writing for *The Territorial Enterprise.* He went on to write stories—published as fact—that he made up entirely.

Perhaps his most famous fake news piece was "The Petrified Man," in which he wrote convincingly about the discovery of a man, said to have been dead a hundred years, who had turned to stone during his long nap.

Twain wrote:

> *"The people of the neighborhood volunteered to bury the poor unfortunate, and were even anxious to do so; but it was discovered, when they attempted to remove him, that the water which had dripped upon him for ages from the crag above, had coursed down his back and deposited a limestone sediment under him which had glued him to the bed rock upon which he sat, as with a cement of adamant, and Judge S. refused to allow the charitable citizens to blast him from his position."*

There had been, at the time, a general mania surrounding the alleged discoveries of "petrified" men, and his real purpose was to make fun of it. And Twain, who seemed to live on the frontier in a state of perpetual bemusement, left clues that careful readers of the piece might have noted, had they attempted to imitate the supposed placement of the mummy's hands, a position which can only be described as the "nanner, nanner" configuration.

A decade after, in a speech given to the Monday Evening Club in Hartford, Connecticut, Twain warned about the perils of news in general: "… the trouble is that stupid people—who constitute the grand overwhelming majority of this and all other nations—do believe and are molded and convinced by what they get out of a newspaper, and there is where the harm lies."

Instead of quashing the ridiculous, Twain's piece helped carry the petrified man sensation to even greater peaks of absurdity.

The Territorial Enterprise was, in retrospect, a kind of fake news academy. James W. Townsend, a colleague of Twain's, went on to found *The Union* newspaper in Grass Valley, California. He was known as "Lying Jim" and described by his former Enterprise editor as: "a unique specimen, by all odds the most original writer and versatile liar that the West Coast, or any other coast, ever produced."

Townsend, while trying to build an audience for his newspaper, allowed himself to invent an entire town, populated with a mayor and city council, with killings and robberies, lawsuits, railroad accidents, and buzzing townsfolk; "Every last one of which he coined out of his own brain."

Almost exactly a hundred years after Twain wrote about petrified men and Townsend was inventing an alternative world, the *Enterprise* struck again when editor Bob Richards published a fake story that camel races would be held in Virginia City. To everyone's surprise, a rival newspaper arrived on the day of the fake race with actual camels, unraveling the story, but also sparking a tradition that carries on to this day, and which now includes ostrich and zebra races, complete with jockeys.

In 1835 the otherwise respectable *New York Sun* published a story claiming that an English astronomer had found life on the moon. Readers were told that the moon, seen through a powerful telescope, was a kind of garden party for unicorns, man-bats, and two-legged beavers.

And the undisputed champion of fake news must be Orson Welles for his 1938 radio show "War of the Worlds," which terrified tens of thousands into believing that Martians were rampaging around with heat-rays and poisonous gas.

Fake news is as old as storytelling. Plato warned about it. But in the bait-and-switch tempest of modern information exchange, and in an era when almost any bizarre claim might seem somehow plausible, it can be nearly impossible to discern the difference.

Dinner with Steve

I don't know why it should be that late last night, while I was riding with TE Lawrence into the fires of Damascus, and only shortly after he had discovered the horrors of the Turkish Hospital, that I would have occasion to reminisce about dining with my father.

It might have been his devotion to all things Lawrence, and memories of a rainy afternoon in San Francisco where we sat together in a dilapidated theater watching Peter O'Toole flog his camel into the redoubts of Aqaba. More precisely, it was the dinner afterward, at a poorly lit, under-attended, and handsomely formal Italian restaurant where he assured me that everyone, up to and including the waiter, was a La Cosa Nostra hitman.

To an impressionable mind, my father's storytelling was inclusive and engaging, and as I pored into a chicken Alfredo, my head stuffed with images of Michael Corleone gunning down Captain McCluskey and that smarmy worm Sollozzo, I was convinced that at any minute we might be interrupted by gunfire, overturned tables, and spilled spaghetti.

What fun.

It is important to track this back, to build the narrative on precise points. It isn't just "Dinner with Steve" that I am trying to deconstruct, after all, but something of myself. It's a difficult feat, I realize, but by taking something apart we often learn more about how it was built.

So. Imagine a sweltering summer day in Burbank, California, heat-wave mirages rising from the asphalt, and a Bob's Big Boy, circa 1977. I might have been six, so the precise human complexities that triggered this event are mysterious, but I do recall with crystal clarity my father announcing: "Alright, kids, are you ready to have some fun?" After ushering us out of the booth, which happened to be on the other side of the window from a gigantic smiling Big Boy outside, Steve, with aplomb, poured all three of our very big untouched milkshakes out over the table. Not entirely satisfied with the mess, he dribbled some fries over the top. Stepping back to admire *that* work, but still not entirely pleased, he squirted some ketchup into the mix and then dumped the remainder of our trays on top of the soup. "Wasn't that great?" he asked loudly, looking around with a slightly mischievous wink and decidedly *not* seeking general approval, then took us by the hands and led us out of the restaurant, past the Big Boy, and into the steaming world.

I have held that image in my mind for nearly forty years: giant milk-shakes slopping over the edge of the table like molten, malted sludge. I was much too young then to understand, or appreciate, that Dinner with Steve was going to become a lifelong adventure.

When my parents divorced—the marriage itself lasting approximately eight minutes—Steve became, and remained almost until his death, a dedicated bachelor. Because he was also a professional pilot, and not least because he sincerely despised any domestic chore whatsoever, Steve dined out for almost every meal in his adult life, and thereby became the terror of restaurants—good and bad—across North America, Europe, South America, and Asia.

Once, in Korea, my colleagues and I were refused service at a series of restaurants in the industrial dump of Pohang by virtue of being U.S. Marines—the managers bracing themselves in the threshold while women with cleavers shrieked in the background. My colleagues were naturally insulted and upset, but I was quite resigned to the terror I noted in the proprietor's eyes—sympathetic even, by virtue of having already had this experience while trying to dine in America with my dad.

Steve, who was capable of enormous and overwhelming passions, also thought of himself as a kind of civilianized Great Santini. At the very least, he had a Santiniesque approach to life, uncompromising, unapologetic, full-throttle, and thrill seeking. He was incapable of playing cribbage with his devoted parents, but he could perform a Split S or an Immelmann Turn in a Pitts Special, par excellence. He could not mow his lawn, but he could skydive, scuba dive, earn a type-rating in an L-39, or ride his Harley to Sturgis. He could pilot a Garden ketch in a Beaufort 9, or land a Boeing 777 in raging crosswinds at night, but he could not wash dishes.

In descending order, he loved his kids, he loved to fly, and he loved to dine. It was the uncompromising, unapologetic, full-throttle, part of him that could turn a simple crab salad at a restaurant in Pago Pago, Samoa, into a perfectly projected, center-stage dissertation on the unacceptable nature of "this plate full of assholes and eyeballs staring at me." And there was a café in Boulogne, France, where he denounced the pâté as a "very poor Gallic interpretation of a duck turd." These gems, always delivered in Whitmanesque exuberance—as a barbaric yawp across the rooftops of the world—have stayed with me.

It wasn't merely the ever-present, nerve-damaging potential for an embarrassing display from Steve, but often the guestlist itself that turned a simple meal into an event. At table there might be, at any one time, and sometimes together: a Vegas-show dancer; a daytime television actor; an actual Reno mafioso; a World War II German U-boat engineer; a strange multimillionaire who lived in a series of flood-damaged cars and dated only See's Candy Women; a movie stuntman; a disgraced diplomat; a celebrity hairdresser; and/or a Navy SEAL commander. And pilots. Always pilots. Test pilots, airline pilots, Korean War combat aces, anyone who had ever touched the throttle in a B-17, glider pilots, hot-air-balloon pilots, even radio-control and drone pilots.

Assemblies of this nature soon commandeer the full attention of a restaurant, particularly at happy hour, and an objective observer would locate Steve in the center of it all, holding court, simultaneously laughing, yelling well-timed profanities, flirting with waitresses, and objecting to the temperature of his enchilada. But even without an audience of friends and acquaintances, Steve found ways to become the center of every patron's dining event. If the table wobbled, it became an Olympic steeplechase contest to find an acceptable arrangement. If someone was smoking a cigarette four blocks away he would proclaim to the entire dining room that there was, in fact, a crematorium next door to the restaurant, and the smoke they were smelling was actually ash from Aunt Gertrude's sad reduction in the oven. And so it went. Always.

Dining was also a convenient substitute for religious inculcation. When we lived in Texas, Steve, ever-mindful of his standing as a single father in the community, would haul my sister and me away on Sunday mornings. It was a staged event, timed to coincide with the neighbors leaving dutifully for church. We would wave to each other from our driveways, but our church was a Chinese restaurant in Arlington, where we discussed Steve's particularly spacious and accommodating beliefs over Mongolian beef and sweet-and-sour pork.

Thanksgiving was often in a Mexican restaurant, Christmas at the Tick Tock in North Hollywood (with sticky rolls to go). Once, after rude service at the landmark Liberty Belle Saloon in Reno—and the requisite and always high-profile storming out—Steve called in a holiday reservation for a party of thirty. He followed up, on the day of, by calling repeatedly to inform the staff that the party was running late, until nobody showed at all.

I could go on: there were the M-80s he dropped in the toilet of a restaurant in Hawaii, returning to our table to wait out the inevitable *warooomph* in the plumbing. The night he ordered the entire dessert cart at the Savoy in London. An embarrassing dustup at a Michelin-rated restaurant in Boston when he demanded to know how anyone in the free world could afford the menu. His anti-imperial display at Tres Hombres in Reno, when he stood with a margarita (on the rocks, no salt), tapped his glass with a knife, and enjoined the dining room to participate in a heartfelt salute and declaration of loyalty to Pancho Villa.

Of course, this behavior was not limited to restaurants and eateries. He related to me once his fondness for issuing "stack calls," wherein he would journey deep into the hallowed stacks of a library, find a niche, and begin to deliver a series of loud, very disturbing, ape-like soundings from the bowels of scholarship. When we saw the movie *Full Metal Jacket* he jumped out of his seat while the credits rolled, ran to the front of the theater and began yelling and gyrating like a deranged veteran. Or a simple madman. If you didn't know him, you wouldn't know it was neither. Today, he would likely be arrested.

Some of this, or maybe all of it, was mere showmanship, I think, a certain delight at dominating center stage, no matter how embarrassing the spectacle. And I should emphasize that he was not malicious. A showman yes, a thoughtless jerk, sometimes, but he never wanted to hurt anyone. He was enjoying life on his own terms, as he understood it, and as he measured himself against the absurdities he understood perfectly. I think he was largely unaware of the embarrassment his outbursts sometimes caused, and in any case was unaffected by whatever trepidation or humiliation might be assumed by those in his company.

Life was too big for a merely emotional response to his flamboyance. That was also his defense, and he came by it honestly and naturally. Whether it was his parents (those models of Greatest Generation dignity) his children, the endless parade of girlfriends, or just friends, he was a live and dangerous wire to carry around in public. And I think there was a reason. I'll tell it even as it hurts, because I know my own culpability, because fathers and sons disagree, and sometimes fight, and precious time is lost—sometimes forever—while they sandbag their own ridiculous positions: *I think he was a kind of genius, and I think he was intensely lonely.*

What is critical, as I drill into the past, is to remind myself that there was good-natured joy in the things he touched and the proselytization of his passions. If he took a shine to Ford 9N tractors—which might last for weeks—the world would know about it, and it was easy to earn a dismissal, an impatient wave of the hand, if one failed to enlist in the cause. He wanted loyal partners in his obsessions and, much like Lawrence, he could not suffer fools or mere dilettantes who lacked his passion, his fixations and his visions.

There is another word for this, megalomania, but I reject its application to Steve as I continue to expunge and harden myself to the trite and altruistic declarations of our decidedly milquetoast culture. As embarrassing and aggravating as he sometimes was, I have learned that we must suffer the eccentricities of genius if we are to know anything about our species, to measure ourselves against the pervasive weaknesses of our time. Where once I suffered, cringing as he carried an undercooked plate of food through the batwing doors into the kitchen, and endured the time-freezing argument that ensued, I now pound my chest and celebrate a life that simply refused to be treated normally.

My father was a friend and confidant of record-setting aviator Jackie Cochrane and her tycoon husband, Floyd Odlum, accomplished Americans both. He was often a guest at their C-O Ranch in Indio, California, and he once bequeathed to me the sum total of knowledge he received from them: *Do not settle for less. Ever.*

And I think we can learn something from that, and maybe, by taking it to heart, we can do something, however small, about improving the mind-numbing and safety-orange conditions that pervade our daily lives. I say this passionately, yet mindful of the potential for excess, and still a bit jealous that it was my sister, and not me, who sat at Eisenhower's desk on the C-O, while Floyd paddled around the gigantic pool on an inflatable raft answering an array of deck-side telephones.

This deconstruction is as necessary as it is endless. I tug on the merest thread and the sweater just gets bigger. And bigger. But these days, when I think of Dining with Steve, I think less of the embarrassing and outrageous sagas, and more of our last meal together, when he flew my wife and me to Catalina, greasing a perfect approach to the oddly sloping and disconcerting airfield at KAVX, Avalon, on Catalina.

We took the shuttle down to Avalon proper, Steve holding forth about the genius of Harry Flashman and a burgeoning obsession with Teddy Roosevelt's adventures in the Amazon; and we strolled the harbor, where he waxed about the landmark Catalina Casino, reminiscing about the perfection of the parquet floors in the ballroom—where he had once danced the jitterbug in a rented tuxedo.

He was in the mind of Jack Nicholson that day as we walked along the quay; Steve hauling up scenes from *The Shining* as we enjoyed the stroll. And when we were seated at a crab shack for lunch he braced the waiter in a perfect Nicholson impression: "Hi, Lloyd," he said, "A little slow tonight, isn't it?"

I think it was that trip, and that dining experience—which was strangely uneventful—where I was surprised to learn that my father loved to dance. And that, dear friends, I would give everything I own to have seen. Even once.

The Killing of Ed's Flip Phone

It is with immense pleasure that I am able to announce that actor and comedian Bill Murray has joined the fledgling GACPA: The Global Anti Cell-Phone Alliance. Mr. Murray has jumped aboard with the aplomb befitting his worldwide celebrity, making an early and loud statement about his commitment by launching several cellphones from the Vesuvio Starlight Rooftop Lounge in Carmel, California. Some may see this as a just another celebrity tirade, but that kind of enthusiasm is fundamentally Luddite, and it's clear that Bill is now with us.

I'm aware of a similar event that probably tops Murray's spectacular act of resistance. This incident took place deep in the Mojave Desert, near an old windmill and a cattle tank, while some of the boys and I were making a reconnaissance in force through that savage country.

We had been at it for a few days, had blown most of our enthusiasm early—which is often how these things go—and so the company was tired, the rigs were breaking down, food and fuel were running short, and someone had broken into the wagonmaster's holdout stash of Old Grandad.

So a sudden, revitalized burst of merriment was being enjoyed around the fire, and the sky was filling up with stars. Then the insults started—slowly at first—until suddenly cigars were being stubbed out in the sand and sleeves rolled up. Then the wrassling got underway. Chad caught a folding chair in the face. A table went over. Dust went up into the sky. There was a muffled shout, bodies scrambling away into the darkness, and then gunfire, and silence.

What happened was: Chad got tired of Ed talking on his flip phone when we were supposed to be out amongst the rattlesnakes and rock piles, ringtone-free, re-creating an age when life was enjoyed without jazzy notifications beamed in from satellites in geosynchronous orbit. And I'll say this: the rest of the grubliners and itinerant Toadvines that composed this raggedy-assed company of marauders were getting right sore at seeing Ed with that damn flip phone, acting for all the world like he was Captain James T. Kirk, demanding an immediate beam-up from Scotty back on the *Enterprise*. Who has a flip phone anyway?

So Chad shot Ed's phone. Right through the 5 key.

I was signed on to this guerrilla outfit as an observer, a kind of Sam Damon tromping through China, but after the dust had settled and those who had blown out of camp for safe ground began slinking back to the fire, we righted the table, relit the cigars, and settled down into our ten-dollar camp chairs. The flip phone lay over in the sand beyond the firelight, bleeding out. No one looked at it. And no one said much, but there was a shadowy mirth among the troopers as the fire sawed back and forth and the occasional ember went up to the heavens. The cold Mojave night pressed in around our little fire, and Marty, who'd slept through all of the fighting and the gunfire, began snoring from his bedroll over in the greasewood.

The killing of Ed's flip phone wasn't talked about much in the subsequent years—sleeping dogs and all that—but it was, beyond a doubt, the genesis of an entirely new ritual on these ramshackle expeditions into the desert: the Assassination of Mike's Ugly Garden Gnomes.

Now, please join me in welcoming Bill Murray into the fold.

A Raid for Horseflesh

Last fall, my mother called and dropped a bomb on our house. She asked if I was sitting down. I wasn't, but I did, quickly, because that's what sons do when their mothers start a conversation that way. And if you are a mother reading this, please don't do that.

She was rolling her bed, she said, selling her saddle, and wanted to know if I would take her last good horse. That's heady stuff from a woman who has been horseback from birth, a natural-born daughter of the desert cattle and horse country.

But she's getting older. She can still ride, still loves it, but the horse needs more than she can muster at this stage. I was shocked by the development, but I was also proud of her. She did the incredibly hard work of facing the world the way it actually is, of evaluating her place in it, and then making a decision without deluding herself, without caving in to pride or sentimentality. Not everyone does that. Human reasoning can often spring from a poisoned well of motivations. So score a point for introspection.

We talked. She cried. And honestly, it got a little dusty on my end, too. Maybe it was just the abruptness of it, or the suddenly audible and disconcerting friction of sand pouring through the hourglass, that maddening timepiece that ultimately runs out on us all.

When an era comes to an end like that, the light changes. The moon slides in front of the sun, things go dark, the birds go quiet, and we live for a moment in a strange silvery shade. And then slowly, by increments, the world lights up again. That's how it felt. That's how it still feels.

But I said yes, of course I'd take the horse, and give her a home forever. And she will never leave our family, for all that she represents. I didn't need to think about it.

I don't think of myself as a great horseman. I'm probably average. Maybe worse than that. I've done some incredibly stupid things on horses, been dumped in rivers, on slicks of rhyolite, or pitched without grace into the buckbrush. It's happened more times than I care to remember, and probably reached its zenith during my tour of duty on the horseback outfits of northern Nevada. The new guy in the bunkhouse gets the knuckleheads, rough-string horses, a collection of castoffs and chicken-feeders, straight cowboy horses—which usually means rank, dumb, or both, and always leads to magnificent wrecks out in the sage.

But I love them anyway, and I love to ride, and try to do it without pretending to be Buck Brannaman or Chris Cox, or while regurgitating pithy horse-psychology from the lollipop trainer-of-the-day. Maybe I've developed my own brand of arrogance, but I despise horse-traders and horsey nonsense and that strange confluence of money and dishonesty and self-deception that seems to surround a growing contingent of the equine universe. I just want to ride, and maybe see some good country from the back of a decent horse.

My imagination is problematic in all this because I can't let anything just be what it is. So I had to recast the trip as a "raid for horseflesh," because that sounds sexy, aligns with my intellectual conceits, and most importantly served as an efficient let-off valve for the highly concentrated sorrow of watching my mom bow away from her life's central passion.

And I was lucky. Raiding alone is never fun, and I was able to find an eager partner to ride along. Oh, and he brought his guitar.

We blasted out of Sisters, through Silver Lake and Paisley, down through Lakeview and finally made the old home place, where we scouted canyon petroglyphs, imagined a world long gone, ate like kings, built a bonfire, and Jim played and sang while the fire sawed and the stars came out and I kept an admittedly inebriated eye fixed on my dear old mom.

In the morning, early, we loaded the horse. Mom cried. Maybe we all did a little bit. And then we drove out, a few miles of dirt road to the hardball where we made the long turn north, the horse riding quietly in the back, the sun just throwing light out over the desert.

It was a good winter on the home range. The mountains are still holding snow on the peaks, and the valley basins are greener than I've seen them in years. It was so good, so brilliant, that I feel a little possessive of it all, a little guarded about sharing it with anyone just now.

So forget what I said. I made it all up. Whatever plans you might have, don't go there. The great basin in spring is a horrendous place. The mountains are ugly. The hot springs are cold. The sky isn't blue and the meadowlarks don't sing.

And anyway, I already took the last good horse.

A Meditation, with Horses

We don't make much of Christmas anymore. Each year the tree gets smaller and we put up fewer lights. Mostly, we just fall behind the season. By mid-May the last of the late Christmas cards usually come in, bloodstained and dusty, like the final dispatches from some epic frontier battle—*big village, come quick, bring packs.* The cards, which mean well, are always full of suggestions that events have overtaken the writers, and are a subtle mix of understated regret mixed with cautious, spiny optimism.

And anyway, I've eaten bad Chinese food on more Christmas Eves than I'd like to admit, which has had a cumulative effect on my store of holiday enthusiasms.

This morning I woke up late from a good sleep, the kind of sleep that is hard to get unless you have already died. Waking—a thing that happened like a slow trip to the surface in a diving bell full of echoes—I realized my sleep was a cousin to the kind of sleep my grandfather embraced one morning in a Reno motel room, and was never seen again.

I imagine him then, wracked and already cadaverous, sitting up in bed with a strange smile and reaching out with those spindly white arms, uttering a final, almost ecstatic "Oh," and falling back on the bed. I'd like to think it happened that way, but I know it didn't.

Somehow I got dressed. I made my first cup of tea and resisted a sudden impulse to watch the Queen's annual dose of holiday platitudes to the Commonwealth. Instead, I sat down in the kitchen window with a steaming mug and realized that every one of my joints has settled into a kind of permanent ache.

That aching, of course, portends a long degenerative slide into other inevitable aches and pains. I thought of various deserts and jungles and city streets where I have sacrificed my body to miserable marches and overblown notions of duty that never actually ended up going anywhere.

There is a cure for this, which is a better exercise program, but instead I watched the dogs, out by the henhouse, running laps in the snow. I was still in the diving bell and struggling for self-possession because the alternative was forcing myself into artless yoga poses on a cold wood floor.

It snowed last night but not much. This morning the sky was blue with fast moving puffs of cloud above the ponderosas. On this butte, where we live, we are always between weather events, but I take my cues from the birds. It bothers me that I don't have names for them all. I admire those little birds because they refuse the daily temptation to go internal. This morning they were hopping around on the rocks by the frozen creek in our yard, having a discussion I couldn't understand.

Maybe they are finches. I want to call them warblers but that's not right. I should know what they are called. I should be better than that. I should see a bird and say, "Well, friend, that's a red-billed ox-pecker" with authority. I wonder where those little birds go at night and how they explain things to each other in the morning.

Two nights ago, I was reading late under the small cone of a lamp in my study, when two Canada geese swept over the house. First I heard their wings brushing the air. It was *that* quiet, and they were *that* close to the window. There was silence and then the wings and then that honking which is a primordial song of happiness in flight.

Because I am often awake in the wee small hours I am aware of the nightlife in our woods. I hear the cat jumping onto the porch, fawns mewling. I hear a lone baritone frog who somehow survives single digit temperatures, and sometimes a wistful pack of coyotes cracking open a portal to the underworld. My favorite is an owl that suddenly starts talking to nobody and waits patiently while nobody answers.

The owl reminds me of a man I saw once in the British Museum. He was standing next to a portrait bust of Ramses II and having an animated conversation with himself. He would talk at length, then fold his arms across his chest to listen, and because he occasionally laughed he seemed to be enjoying the witty rejoinders of someone utterly invisible to the rest of the world.

I am often overwhelmed by a desire to sleep outside which is both a courtship and a natural cure for ailments of the mind.

Once, on the banks of the Susquehanna River, I had a moment of absolute clarity while standing next to a Polish poet who later became famous. For just a moment I understood, perfectly, a monk's desire to live in silence. I don't know if it was the poet, or the humidity, or the languid movement of the river in mid-summer. I was reading a lot of Dostoevsky in those days and it's possible I had simply walked into a seductive ambush.

I contemplated my own vow of silence at that moment but instead I went for a hike in Ricketts Glen State Park. Then I wrote a bad poem about an imaginary hermit that I was forced to recite in front of a crowd of people dressed in Harris Tweed, including a mildly pompous professor who lived self-consciously in a barn and serially mispronounced the otherwise beautiful Spanish word "Nevada."

It's winter, but just now, down at the barn, the horses are standing asleep in pockets of warm sunlight. They have eaten, and their bellies are full and warm.

This Christmas morning I am tempted to join them, to find my own place in the bright patches of snow between the trees. I would stand as still as they do, my eyes half-closed, my head hanging ever so slightly. I can imagine doing that for hours, and maybe even falling into a standing dream of the kind that horses have in moments like this, which can only be of golden pastures under the bluest skies, and swirling clouds of summer songbirds. I would happily stand there with them this morning without moving at all, falling easily into the same equine dream, and without even needing to breath.

From Backstraps to Beets: A Hunter-Gatherer in the Digital Age

"A human being should be able to change a diaper, plan an invasion, butcher a hog, conn a ship, design a building, write a sonnet, balance accounts, build a wall, set a bone, comfort the dying, take orders, give orders, cooperate, act alone, solve equations, analyze a new problem, pitch manure, program a computer, cook a tasty meal, fight efficiently, die gallantly. Specialization is for insects."

—Robert Heinlein

Many of us have a strong interest in knowing where our food comes from. My own interest runs toward growing and hunting our food because I see those efforts as critical priorities in the exercise of free-will and self-reliance in a digital culture with decidedly different priorities.

But even if you don't share my interest, it would seem difficult to argue that, as a practical matter, knowing how to grow and harvest one's own food, and how to process and preserve it, isn't just as important as knowing how to drive a car, read a book, or buy a plane ticket.

The efforts we are making to that end, here on our tiny ranch on the eastern slope of the Cascades, aren't easy. They aren't even cost-effective. Given that a McWhopper goes for about dollar, I can have a pile of pizzas delivered anytime I want, and frozen turkey by the metric ton is available at Costco every day of the week—why bother with the time and expense of building a greenhouse or raising chickens? And worse, after years of costly and determined effort, we still get the vast majority of our food from a local grocer.

All of which troubles me.

That kind of dependency troubles me because we are never much more than three missed meals away from the collapse of law and order—proof of which can be seen on CNN after virtually any natural or political disaster around the world. But even here, in a mostly secure nation, it's inescapably true, for the vast majority of us, that without our local grocer, and the complex and astonishingly fragile system that keeps food coming into the aisles, we would eventually, in all likelihood, starve to death.

That's dramatic, of course, but probably not as far-fetched as it sounds, given the unpredictable, turn-on-a-dime nature of life on planet earth, and more importantly it serves as a constant reminder that a life of utter dependence is a sucker's game.

Particularly when it comes to food. Industrial food producers …

> *"… will grow, deliver, and cook your food for you and (just like your mother) beg you to eat it. That they do not yet offer to insert it, pre-chewed, into your mouth is only because they have found no profitable way to do so."*
>
> —Wendell Berry

One challenge of writing about our personal efforts to grow and harvest food is that the topic falls easily into the habits of a reader's pre-conditioning, and therefore elicits a lot of eye-rolling. That pre-conditioning is accomplished by means of consumer-marketing imagery that we have absorbed into our tissue like radiation poisoning after decades of internet, television, and radio advertising. It is so pervasive, in fact, that now we barely even notice that all of that promotional carpet-bombing is designed to compel our surrender into dependency.

Just eat the Doritos, and forget about growing kale.

We are, many of us, walking around with a veteran consumerist's thousand-yard stare, which can be seen clearly in the aisles of any Target or WalMart, where the shell-shocked and emotionally flat-lined queue up daily to buy mostly disposable products manufactured by sweatshop slaves in Chittagong and Rangoon. Especially when there is a "Fire Sale," or its cousin the "Closeout Sale," or my personal favorite, the "Blowout Sale."

Sometimes, the imagery is even amusing. A mention of gardening might, for example, conjure images of the Blue-Haired Gardening Gestapo—those mean little old ladies who lead community garden tours wearing badges denoting their frocking as "Master Gardeners"—who go about tsk-tsking anyone who hasn't bloomed the *Dracula Lotax*, a notoriously difficult orchid, in their own designer arboretum.

Hunting—and firearms in general—comes with its own set of baggage. It's a world where every armchair outdoorsman secretly thinks he's Peter Hathaway Capstick, and seems to attract a strange confluence of Fire-in-the-Belly, Neo-Tribal, Uber-Tactical, Club-Faraday crazies. These are the folks who, virtually without fail, serve to lower the level of any meaningful hunting or gun conversation by swamping it with overheated diatribes about what caliber we should all be shooting, or with epic tales about the main-beam score of their last bull elk.

But I don't hunt for trophies, and I've probably given far too much thought to double tapping the next square-range commando who assails me in a religious pique over the virtues of all things 1911.

At any rate, the hunter-gatherer discussion remains useful, even essential, if we care about building meaningful resiliency into our lives, or merely wish to avoid a complete metamorphosis into oversized insects ordered around by our smartphones.

Here on the Figure 8 Ranch—which we named because naming things has a way of elevating our appreciation for them—we have, over the last few years, made a conscious, challenging, and often frustrating effort to grow, or to hunt, as much of our own food as we reasonably can.

That effort begins in the greenhouse in early spring, when we sow seeds, and ends in the late fall when I head out with a rifle into the woods or onto the high desert to find an elk, or a deer, or both—who I pray, as the Wintu Indians of California thought of it, is willing to die for me that day.

My belief in the importance of growing food, I realize now, started long before we ever moved into the woods of central Oregon, and is inextricably linked to the circumstances of my own upbringing.

I was raised on the sagebrush desert of northeastern California, at precisely that point where the northern Sierras form the western boundary of the Great Basin. It was, and remains, a rural and largely ignored part of the country. My mother managed a large garden each summer from which we drew our vegetables; and we raised sheep, cattle, pigs, and chickens for protein. My stepfather worked at the sawmill in town and my mother, when she wasn't churning butter out of cream from our milk cow, raised four kids.

We never had a lot of money, but we never worried about going hungry either.

None of that autobiography is important except that, I think, it demonstrates to some small degree that how we teach our children to live often ends up becoming how they actually live. If no one ever teaches them, for instance, how to grow a vegetable, or to fish for trout, or to hunt a deer, they probably won't be passing those skills on to their own kids, so that within a single generation the bedrock of our long-heralded American self-reliance—growing and harvesting food—is either hanging on by life support or stone-cold dead.

Mostly, and when it is probably more important than ever, I fear that it is dead.

> *"The capacity of people in the cities to do things directly for themselves is extremely limited. They can't produce food. They can't produce building materials or the materials needed for clothing. They're so cut off from the natural sources of their livelihood and so far cut off from fundamental skills, most of them, that they can't directly do much of anything."*
>
> —Wendell Berry

To be sure, there are people out there doing the same thing better, smarter, and more successfully than we are. Some of the people I draw inspiration from, such as the YouTube sensation Wranglerstar, are doing it at a level of intelligence and accomplishment that we can only dream of, given the limitations of our land.

But our own efforts remain relevant because we are probably more like everyone else: forced to keep one foot closer to the grinding centers of population and commerce in order to keep the lights on and the freezers humming.

Even so, and the unavoidable irony notwithstanding, we are still making a genuine effort at food production. And in this endeavor, effort counts. It counts because every failure is instructional to an extreme degree in the enjoyable pursuit of eventually getting it right.

Which is why, when we sat down for dinner not long ago and ate an entire meal consisting of food we had either grown in the garden, or hunted off the rimrock, I felt no small measure of satisfaction. It was a victory for the quieter kind of activism I admire most—the individual taking direct action to responsibly improve their own condition. No petition, no pussyhat, no sandwich board required.

Truth is, I am mostly interested in acts of solitary activism, in the spirit of Thoreau at Walden, or Rick Bass in the Yaak Valley of Montana. Because I no longer have much faith in the gargantuan, faraway, machine-bureaucracy apparatus known as the Federal Government, or its long-term intentions to preserve, protect, and defend the constitution, you won't find me banging a gong in support of one retail political candidate or another. In other words, I have no political home, and staying off the reservation demands that I ride a wide circle, keeping as far as possible from the diseased blankets and steel trappings of the soldiers' fort.

Growing a vegetable can be, and hunting certainly is, political in the eyes of many. So be it. For my wife and me the act of planting seeds, tending a garden, and eventually harvesting a basket of vegetables, or of hunting an elk out of the junipers on the high desert, and finally putting them all together on a plate at our dinner table, is a ballot cast for precisely what matters most to us. It is a vote for intimacy with the details of our own lives, and for the maintenance of our dwindling freedoms.

The Mill Party

I am sentimental about sawmills. That's especially true around Christmas because the Sierra Pacific sawmill, at one time the second largest of its kind in the United States, was also the principal private employer where I was raised—in the sparsely populated northeast corner of California.

My stepfather worked at Sierra Pacific for over twenty years, rolling logs in the millpond, pulling chain, freezing through graveyard shifts in the stacker house, and finally loading long lines of trucks and boxcars on a forklift. Like every man in that industry he worked like a Georgia mule, sometimes seven days a week, and never once did anyone hear him complain.

I often wonder what went through his mind on those long, very cold, and chaotic nights in the lumber mill, or the blistering hot summer days, when just about any place on earth probably felt like a better place to be. And I cherish memories of those dark mornings when, as I lay awake in my warm bed, he came home and slipped into the house like a ghost. I would lie in bed and listen as he quietly stoked the woodstove in the living room, so that when we all got up for school the house would be warm.

Throughout my childhood, our fortunes rose and fell with the vagaries of the timber industry. There were lean times, when my stepfather would bring home a notice on company letterhead from "Red" Emmerson—who had built a small empire of lumber mills across northern California from the ground up—lamenting with sincerity a series of layoffs.

And those days were made still leaner when the sawmill whistle, which blew every day at noon over the town of Susanville, went terribly and awkwardly silent, and we sat on my mother's bed counting out nickels and pennies to pay for school pictures.

My stepdad would make up the difference by feeding out cattle for our neighbors. He would cross the creek below our place—we lived far out of town—on a slippery old two-by-twelve, then walk up the hill to the hay yards where hungry cattle stood covered in ice and bawling, on mornings so cold he had to use a blowtorch to unlock the tractor tires where they had frozen to the ground.

But even in those rougher times there was an abiding sense of local community that bound families together. There was no notion of an aristocracy in our county, no family who wasn't touched directly or indirectly by the fortunes of the mill. We were all in it together, come what may, and we never went hungry.

None of that has ever left me. If anything, those days are so deeply ingrained that I can't smell fresh-sawn lumber without thinking of my stepdad's work clothes hanging in the laundry room, his battered blue hardhat sitting on the dryer next to his worn-out old gloves, or see in my mind's eye the towering decks of timber sitting in the summer sunlight, watered by sprinklers, waiting to be fed into the sawmill.

And there were good times, too. In this season of giving thanks, I am grateful for memories of the Mill Party, a Christmas bash for the sawmill men and their families when the lumber industry was humming, before it was sacrificed to know-it-alls in the special interest and political cabals, then crated up and shipped offshore to support other families, in some other country, somewhere else in the world.

For the Mill Party—which to a young boy was the biggest single event of the holiday season—families would gather at the fairgrounds, hundreds of people in their modest Sunday best, and each child was called up to the front of the room by a huge man dressed as Santa Claus to receive a present.

Santa would draw your name out of a hat, or a box, or whatever it was, and you walked up there in front of everyone to embrace a gift that not only meant something about Christmas, but about what it meant to live in a community of people who knew what hard times really look like, knew how to spread the wealth when things were better, and worried fiercely about the future of an industry they had invested their lives—and the fortunes of their families—in seeing succeed.

And I can remember those years, which was most of them, when I would ask my parents when the Mill Party was, and they didn't have an answer. As an adult I can see that silence for what it really was, and I am grateful for the strength and the grace they had to shield their children from the worries they carried in their chests like hot, heavy stones.

The mill is gone now, mostly torn down to a rusty shell of its former self. It is the way of things. But I will never be able to pass that place between the train tracks and the Susan River without hearing the noon whistle, or remembering that long walk down the aisle toward an exhausted lumberman dressed as Santa Claus, who handed me a present with a smile. And I know now that whatever it might have been when I was a small boy, a Tonka truck or a brace of silver six-shooters, I will be unwrapping that gift for the rest of my life.

Death in the Creekbed

"The danger of civilization, of course, is that you will piss away your life on nonsense."

—Jim Harrison

In a consumer society, where so much of what we require for daily life forces us into roles of utter dependence upon complex, fragile, and unaccountable systems, there are few remaining outlets that allow us at least the illusion of self-sufficiency. Hunting is one of them. While it is one thing to be a subsistence hunter in the Alaskan interior, where hunting often remains a fact of daily life, it is entirely another to be a seasonal hunter in the lower forty-eight where, for all practical purposes, the next meal is waiting conveniently at the corner market. So I'm under no romantic illusions about the practical necessity of hunting. Said another way, I *know* it's not strictly necessary to hunt for my meat, but I choose to do it anyway because I believe it remains an important pursuit of the body, mind, and soul.

I feel compelled to hunt precisely because it is a respite from raw consumerism, that other life where we are both dependent on the system that provides for us, and walled off from the entire sequence of events necessary to bring meat—or even vegetables—from the field to our dinner plates. I feel compelled to hunt for many of the same reasons I feel compelled to raise vegetables—because raising and securing food brings intimacy with the details of my life.

I believe that sort of intimacy is important for perspective, and for a better understanding of cause and effect, and better informs my views in discussions about how our descendants are going to live on this planet generations from now. I feel compelled to hunt for protein because killing an animal in the wild, and doing the work necessary to bring that meat home to my family still resonates in my mind as the important work of a male adult. Hunting an animal, and taking its life with respect and with gratitude, to provide life for my own family, blows out the X-Ring in the target of my life.

Killing animals is not an unusual activity for me—slaughtering chickens, hogs, sheep, and cattle were principal activities of my upbringing. But nothing compares to being out on the land with a rifle. Nothing else I have experienced even comes close to the solemn thrill of finding, tracking, and finally putting an elk down in the brush with a rifle shot.

This fall I drew a nominally terrific deer tag out east, which is to say east of our homeplace here on the Figure 8, near the John Day Wilderness of Oregon. I spent two days scouting that country and saw exactly two deer: a faun and a doe. And because deer tags there are abundant, and I knew that hunting deer after opening day would resemble an Elmer Fudd cartoon with hundreds of yahoos, and their assortment of ATVs and side-by-sides chugging relentlessly around in the woods—

a ridiculous spectacle which puts so much pressure on already reduced deer populations that the experience is essentially and full of misery. And so, happily, I decided to skip deer season altogether and focus on elk.

I was fortunate that way because an old colleague, Doug Kresky, had procured deprivation tags for the North Point Ranch, owned by a cattle rancher named Don Cavaletto. Don runs cattle and farms wheat on a sizeable chunk of country in the heart of Oregon elk habitat. And because the elk herds on his property and the surrounding country are abundant, the state of Oregon issues deprivation tags to reduce the size of the elk herds on his property. This is necessary for those in the business of agriculture—people raising food for everyone else—because a herd of three hundred elk grazing in a field overnight can cause tremendous damage and financial loss to anyone trying to grow a crop, or whose cattle herds depend on the same grass. Deprivation hunting is a good practice, and from what I can tell it is well-managed by the state; the downstream effect is lower prices in the supermarket, and a bonus opportunity for hunters like me looking to escape the Hanna-Barbera version of hunting in the modern West. It's a win-win-win, for landowner, hunter, and consumer.

This is not trophy hunting. Not that I wouldn't love to mount a gigantic 7x7 bull on the wall above our fireplace, but it isn't what drives me. I want meat, pure and simple. But even without paying thousands of dollars for a guided trophy-bull hunt, a mere deprivation cow tag doesn't pencil out. When you sit down to do the math on how much you are paying for the meat—that is, after buying a decent rifle, decent ammunition, a hunting license and tags, necessary gear such as a bedroll, binos, fuel, food to eat on the hunt, and possibly a professional butcher if you do not have the skill or capacity to process the meat at home, it is quite likely you are paying more per pound than you would for decent beef at a supermarket.

But it tastes better than supermarket protein, and more importantly, writing good poetry has never paid much either.

And the truth is, I love to hunt. I love the early mornings, the camaraderie in a group of good hunters, the sense of individual purpose in the vast wilderness, the requirement to find some finer level of attunement with the natural surroundings, the participation in a cycle of life, and the employment of a skillset that sets one aside from the madding crowd of pure booger-eating consumers waiting in the check-out line and reading tabloid headlines next to the breath fresheners. I take no small pride in saying yes, indeed, I am a hunter. I kill meat for my family.

So last week Doug drove up from Paso Robles, California, where he lives with his wife on a vineyard and raises grapes for wine. He brought his youngest son Keith with him. Doug has taken his sons on hunting trips around the Western states, but they had never hunted elk, and I was privileged to be invited to share in the gift of deprivation tags on country I had never hunted. And on Tuesday morning, early, we left the Figure 8 hauling a horse trailer with our gear, driving east through Redmond, Prineville, Dayville, and the tiny hamlet of Mount Vernon—home of world champion rodeo cowboy Trevor Knowles—on a winding and mostly valley-bottom highway that traces the banks of the John Day River.

It is a big, empty, country.

In Mt. Vernon we gassed up and turned north through the Wallowa-Whitman National Forest toward Pendleton, home of the world-famous Pendleton Round-Up and the Hamley Saddle Company. We made a short stop in Pendleton at the Oregon Department of Fish and Wildlife office to pick up our tags, where we also met a decidedly obese and incidentally limited thinker who insulted my friends for being from California, was chock-full of the twangy bluster of the blissfully ignorant, and claimed to have been working as an outfitter in the country for three or four hundred years. I forget which.

There isn't much we can do about that sort of unfortunate failure of intellect, or just plain manners, in a man fair-met in a public space, except weather the stupidity by taking the high road, rolling our eyes behind his back, and hoping humanity will offer up some better version of people in the not-too-distant future. But that tension toward all things California is also a real thing in many parts of the more rural West, even when it is ultimately stupid, rude, and self-defeating.

And it wasn't lost on me—as we shifted uncomfortably in the ODFW office and waited for the new secretary to sort out the tags—that just on the other side of the road sat the sad result of over two hundred years of disgraceful treatment of the indigenous people of the Columbia Plateau. Forty feet from where we stood next to Cowboy Dipshit in the ODFW office was a plot of housing for the Confederated Tribes of the Umatilla (Umatilla, Cayuse, and Walla Walla tribes) which—translated into real terms—means a third-world pile of wrecked mobile homes with cars on blocks, piles of shrapnel, swing sets turned upside down on dead grass, stunted and broken trees, blown-out old burn barrels, and a distinct aura of poverty, neglect, and hopelessness.

And all of this despite the Wildhorse Resort and Casino, which is nearby, run by the tribes, and meant to pour money back into a community that needs every advantage it can possibly leverage to overcome two centuries of spite and racial hatred.

But that sad state of affairs is a long thread which is better not pulled on here. I noted that the construction flagging crews—there was considerable roadwork taking place on Highway 11 between Pendleton and Milton-Freewater, were native—which was at least encouraging in the entrepreneurial sense.

We arrived in the small city of Milton-Freewater greeted by an assortment of public statuaries depicting frogs in various antics. This is a result of either Milton-Freewater's nickname, Muddy-Frogwater, or the efforts of a former mayor to make lemonade out of lemons and give the town some claim to a sense of humor. It's hard to say which. Milton-Freewater is an agricultural town, which means it is full of churches, taco trucks for the armies of Mexican laborers who pass through to pick apples, cherries, plums, or peas, and tractor dealerships every eight or nine feet. The city itself isn't particularly appealing to the eye or the sensibility, and anyone with a discerning mind has the sense that methamphetamine mopes do a brisk and heart-wrenching business among Milton-Freewater's shifty and restless youth.

From town we made our way out toward the North Point Ranch, through rolling orchards and out again onto the dryland wheat fields, now in stubble and dotted with towering silos and grain elevators, up a narrow and pot-holed Birch Creek Road until we made the ranch gate at the foot of the mountains and the steep draws leading up into the towering, piney heights of Government Mountain. From the gate we drove down into an oak studded draw and pulled up in front of an old shop building and some sorely beaten sorting corrals, where two saddle-horses were tied to the rail, a cattle-hauler was backed up to the loading chute, and the cowboys were busy weaning calves off their mothers and running them into the truck with whistles, curses, threats, and hot-shots.

Which meant, for me, that I felt instantly at home.

After introductions all around we made our camp inside the shop next to an enormous John Deere combine parked inside against the coming winter, set up our kitchen in a cloud of box-elder bugs excited to have company, and lit a fire in the stove. The stove was essentially two fifty-five-gallon drums welded atop each other, with a flue held together with baling wire and a spot-welded support system, a structure cavorting at various angles until it reached a hole in the ceiling, some thirty feet above us. But Terrell, the six-foot-four, three-hundred-forty-pound ranch manager who was covered in cowshit, dust, and good humor, assured us that the stove would put off enough heat to drive us out of the shop, which later turned out to be an accurate assessment of its efficiency. Terrell also mentioned that he had just seen thirty elk in a different draw just up the road, and seemed to be encouraging us to go shoot them right then and there lest we lose the opportunity.

The idea was intriguing, but the sun was tilting into dusk and after a long drive I wasn't up to a night full of gutting elk, quartering them in the moonlight, and hauling them out. This was elk country, after all, and I felt confident we would find them in the morning without much trouble and would probably have our cow tags filled by lunchtime.

And why rush it? A hunting trip is meant to be enjoyed as much as it is meant to harvest meat, because it is the thrill of the hunt—far more than the kill—that releases something ancient in our DNA and gifts us with stories of prowess—and no shortage of outright lies—to share with those who would listen far into the future.

Once I had my bedroll set up on a cot, I yanked a beer from the cooler and went outside to watch the cow work. It has never failed to amaze me how much good work good cowboys can do with limited equipment and/or terrible conditions, and in this case I was pondering the dry-rot in the loading chute that just kept taking repeated abuse by a thundering roll of stupid cows wedging themselves in the squeeze or turning around in the chute.

It's been said that you can measure the money behind a ranch by whether or not the gates all close properly, but I've never seen an actual working cattle outfit where that was even remotely true. Most of the working gear is just hammered back into shape and held together with baling twine, which was the case on the North Point—as it has been on every ranch I have ever cowboyed on. Around the sorting corrals of real cow outfits there are always a few scour-splattered five gallon buckets full of squashed beer cans, random piles of old ear tags, various objects of uncertain origin discarded for unknown reasons, heaps of unrecognizable cast-off wood, iron, and twine, and in this case, there was an elk hide draped over one of the fence panels and a row of ravens sitting on that with infinite wisdom and impertinence shining in their big black eyes.

The downside to arriving when we did was that we would not be getting any sleep. With their calves weaned off, cows don't shut up for a couple of days; instead they stand around bawling at the world for the cruelty of their station within it. Sitting inside a steel shop with a hundred cows on the other side of the wall made for quite the old-West serenade as we sat around in ruined plastic chairs by lamplight, sorting our gear, stoking the fire with wood hauled from the Figure 8, drinking cold beer and a little whiskey, and watching the evening light give way to darkness in the draw.

And still I slept like a child, which is a rare thing for me.

In the morning we rose, and shook the bugs off our bedrolls with the cows still bawling in the dark. Doug made a fine egg-and-potato breakfast on the two-burner. I boiled water for tea. We took turns in the privy out in the yard, which was really just an old Andy Gump stationed over a small hole in the ground, and so overwhelmed by alder bugs and hornets it turned a man's morning ablutions into an Olympic-style feat of courage and endurance.

It was frisky in the morning moonlight, though not altogether cold, and the shop was more or less filled with smoke because we'd closed the towering doors (only recently replaced after the combine sheared them off in the parking exercise) and clamped the damper too hard on the stove overnight. Old contraptions like that take some time to negotiate with, but there was absolutely nothing about the challenge of our camp in that shop that I didn't love. By the end of our hunt I had that old stove dialed, and could have lived in the shop all winter, bugs and all. I've certainly lived in worse places.

With a cup of tea steaming on a table with stacked paint cans for legs at either end, I laced up my hunting boots and pulled out the one piece of camouflage gear I now wear when hunting: an old quilt-lined jacket (with the stuffing coming out in places) that I picked up for fifteen bucks on a sale rack that says "Deer Killer" on the label. It is a terrible jacket in a lot of ways, particularly when wet, but it has been lucky for me, stuffs into my pack without too much heartache, and I'm not willing to part with it.

Also, I don't go in for much of the Gucci hunting-gear craze. For one thing, I'm mindful that our grandparents made plenty of great hunts wearing red plaid, and for another thing, Chief Plenty Coup of the Absaroka went out of his way to condemn the white man for always wearing too many clothes and building fires that were wasteful. That's a strange combination of influences but I've hunted with guys who paid thousands of bucks for their hunting outfits—the newest ensemble from KUIU for instance—and even some who believed putting all of their clothes in scent-free bags overnight was going to make them better hunters.

Mostly, it just doesn't—which would come as no surprise to old Plenty Coup.

So I generally hunt in Wranglers and the Deer Killer, and since I've harvested three elk in the last five years maybe I'm not so crazy. I top off my own ensemble with a comfortable and very warm Stormy Kromer my daughter bought me for Christmas, and carry a bloodstained old backpack containing my gutting and skinning knives, a range-finder, water, some rope, marking tape, an extra pair of gloves, and in this case a breakfast burrito wrapped in aluminum foil. And of course I carry good binos, which is my one capitulation to the sporting-goods industry's ferocious exploitation of a largely working-class pursuit. I like Leupold glass because the Gold Ring still means something in terms of service and reliability; and all of my riflescopes are built by them.

My hunting rifle is a .280 Ackley Improved built by Nosler in Bend, Oregon. Through a friend I was fortunate to buy this rifle directly from the gunsmith who built it, shortly after he retired from Nosler, and at a discount even though it had never been fired. It is a lightweight rifle with a wooden stock—which I insist on in a hunting rifle—and is perfect for shouldering around during long days in rugged country. The .280 AI is a flat-shooting, powerful round that will drop virtually anything walking around in North America. It also has an exceptionally moderate recoil, which is something I prefer in all of my rifles. And it shoots sub-MOA, which is probably the most important feature. I like that rifle a lot, and would prefer never to hunt with anything else.

With breakfast down and tea in my mug, we loaded our rifles in the truck, pulled out of the HQ, and headed up in the dark toward Government Mountain, which forms a kind of natural boundary between the North Point and other ranches in the country. At its lower ends, where we started, the country is dryland wheat, wildly sloping hills (driving a tractor over that ground, given the angles, is impressive as hell) giving way to steep and narrow draws where oaks give way to cottonwood and finally ponderosa pine at the heights. What isn't plowed is still in grama grass and shrub.

The road up to Government Mountain is marginal, and we were told in winter it is virtually impassible. The various fields on the lower slopes are marked by oft-repaired two- and three-wire fences, or no fences at all, and while all of it is perfect elk habitat that country is also home to the Walla Walla wolf pack. Terrell, the ranch manager, told us that sighting wolves on the country is not at all unusual, and is rather a kind of running gunfight to protect the calves from predation. But that, too, is a longer string to pull on.

We made our way up the road in the dark—it was light enough to see without headlights—jouncing up a rocky road until we were high above our camp, where we finally parked and got out to start glassing the country for elk.

The short version of this hunt is simple. We glassed all morning. We made some scouting forays into the country. We drove around to the very top of the ranch, got out of the truck, and punched back down to the top of the draws looking for sign, looking for elk on the move, and enjoying the country while learning to read it. On the far edge of the world sat Milton-Freewater, the red lights from an impressive array of windmills giving way to daylight and the occasional soft boom of bird cannons in the thin green swaths of distant orchards. The wind was out of the southwest and mostly warm. We hunted separately, though loosely coordinated, combing through the brush and the rocks and the tops of the draws, looking for water where the elk might congregate, for evidence of beds or fresh spoor, and at one point I encountered a beautiful four-point white tail buck. He stopped and stared at me, and I at him, no more than fifty yards from each other. In the end I watched him bound across the tall grass and over a hummock into the rest of his life.

By noon we had seen no elk, only cattle placidly grazing on the golden forty-degree slopes of the draws. Doug had walked down into the bottoms and made a long scout through the country back to the shop. Keith and I met up in the field, took a short drive into even higher country to see what it might hold, then drove back down to the shop for lunch and a rest.

I sometimes get a sense when hunting. I can't entirely explain it, but there is an otherworldly physical thing that inhabits my body and mind. It whispers that success is near. This is a real experience that has never once failed me. It's true that before a hunt I try to force my thoughts and dreams into a kind of animal reality, where I see and rehearse the possibilities in the field. I see the animal. I see myself on the country. I see us drawn together. I suppose it is my own kind of mental dance around the campfire, my own summoning of the Norse God Ull, my own ancient and resurrected need to summon the powers of chance and skill by the stars so that they might meet together out on the grass or deep in the trees to make a successful hunt.

It is a ritual of the heart and mind and it is a personal ritual that I believe in, so much so that I sometimes doubt the academic interpretations of ancient depictions of hunting. The lessons drawn from the hunting art of antiquity are often imagined by well-intentioned academics who seem to have never hunted for their meat, or personally felt the draw of the animal and its power over the mind, or the power of blood-ritual on the land. The symbols and figures found on ancient cave walls lose their meaning and immediacy by dissertation.

And back here, in the 21st century, we made lunch in the shop from white bread, salami, and Coors Light in a can.

We had a plan for the afternoon, which was to return to the heights and sit on some water holes where we thought, rightly, the elk would travel when they were up from their beds and on the move. So we jounced back up to the top, and then made a slow and deliberate hunt until we were in a good position—spread out over half a mile—to glass the country.

And we were several hours into that when I saw, far down below, a single cow elk emerge from a copse of oak trees and begin wending her way across a field of stubble. I watched her through the glass for quite some time, and watched the trees to see if any other elk would emerge because it is a fact that several hundred elk can be bedded down in the trees and be nearly impossible to see.

And it was about this time that I encountered another of those weird modern hunting puzzles, which is the oddity of humanity making a sudden appearance: just as the elk disappeared into a cleft in the land, a paraglider swung into view, piloting his go-kart on a bright blue parachute through a saddle in the rolling wheat fields.

What a paraglider was doing there, or where he came from, or where he eventually went, is entirely a mystery to me.

But I had seen an elk, which could only mean there were more elk in the offing. And, as the gods would have it, she had made her way to exactly the place that Terrell had told us we would find them. So I moved out to find Doug and Keith and to guide us down.

I found Doug a half-mile away glassing a hillside, but it turned out—in a frustrating text-message exchange in a place where cell-service was either bad or non-existent—that Keith had also seen that lone elk, and had already set off on a desperate long-distance haul down off the mountain and through the bottoms, up again on the other side, across the road, into the stubble, and was now sitting on a herd of fifty elk.

So we vamoosed, made the frustratingly slow drive back around the mountain and finally pulled up on the edge of the road, disembarked, linked up with Keith in the tall grass bordering the stubble, and poked our heads up to see a delightful herd grazing the greenest shoots of winter wheat. There was a beautiful bull standing in the middle of the herd and somewhere to our left a second bull was bugling, a sound that echoed off the stubble and around in the oak bottoms far below.

It was at that moment that I had a strange, discomfiting experience. I felt, fleetingly, as though I were a cavalry soldier peering down at an Indian camp blissfully unaware of our presence. It was a sudden and very hard vision and bothers me still. I will only be able to work out what that might mean—and I believe it means something—with time and reflection.

I shook off the vision and we made a short stalk for better position, crawling into a screening border of tall grass. I surveyed the elk looking for a cow without a calf, and settled on one nearer the far side of the herd. And then we fired.

In retrospect I think we rushed the shots. We crippled both cows instead of dropping them in place, and while the herd scattered, the cows limped slowly down into the cover and safety of the trees, about a hundred yards apart. There was nothing to do then but to sidehill down and find a blood trail, follow it, and finish the job. I found a blood trail and finally found my cow at the exact bottom of the draw, in a wild tangle of oak trees and brush riven through the center by a narrow, deep, and dry creekbed. I stood over her enormous body and talked softly to her, thanking her for her life, and for her courage. And then I finished the job with a single shot from my pistol.

What comes after the kill is nothing but hard work. It was late in the afternoon, turning toward evening, and with two elk down we had decisions to make. In the end we decided to gut them and leave them in the field until morning, when we could quarter them and begin the arduous process of hauling several hundred pounds of meat straight up out of the bottoms. There is always the chance that predators, coyotes or wolves or birds, will get after the meat overnight, but in this case there was very little we could do about it. So I gutted my cow and then coached Keith through his, and we climbed up out of the killing ground in the solid dark covered in blood up to the elbows.

We made it back to camp that night exhausted by a full day of hunting, the exhilaration of the kill, and the very hard work of gutting two large elk in the dark in a Tolkienesque creek-bottom. And in the morning we returned, refreshed, and relieved to find that the predators had left our kills alone—even as a coyote following his nose to our elk scampered off when we arrived.

We spent the next several hours skinning and quartering out our meat, then stacking it on tarps we had decided to use for sleds to pull out the loads. And it is worth mentioning that when we had finished dismembering, we hauled the first loads out on those makeshift travois up a hill which might rival K2 for the steepness. It was an ass-kicker, that first load, and left us with the unhappy prospect of going back down to bring the rest of the meat up. Which is precisely when the toys of modernity and the convenience of contemporary living entered and saved us the hassle: a deus ex machina in the form of Terrell arrived in his side-by-side accompanied by two cowdogs and a cowboy. He was able, by some miracle of skill against gravity, to maneuver that grinding little machine down impossible angles without crashing, load up the rest of the elk, and haul it up.

We brought the meat back to the shop, unwrapped the tarps, then hosed the dirt and the hair off. We drank beer. And then Keith and I took the load down to a freezer owned by a large-scale farmer in Milton-Freewater named David Morris. We had called ahead, and David told us that he would take payment in a thirty-pack of Keystone Light, so we bombed into a convenience store, restocked our own supply of beer, secured the Keystone, and took the meat to the headquarters of David's orchard, where we met David. Which becomes one of the other highlights and bonuses of hunting—the people one meets.

David harvests eight hundred tons of cherries, a like-amount of plums, and several hundred tons of apples each year in his orchards, and gave us some interesting opinions on the people of Milton-Freewater: “They are all liars,” he said, only half-joking, and before launching into a discussion of how his third marriage is working out only two years into the enterprise. We might have known him our entire lives, and we saw him later again that evening, back at the shop, when he came out to the North Point to cut an old beehive out of a tree because the new wife makes decorations out of them. “The things we do for love,” he said.

In the morning we packed up our camp and began the long drive home. We had secured our meat. It was a good, albeit brief, hunt, and I look forward to many more before the sun sets on my ability to tie myself back to the land by participating in the cycles. I hope that day never comes, but it is certain to, and I hope I will have done enough by then to pass on whatever I have learned to someone else who cares as passionately as I do about the conservation of our wildlands and our wildlife. Someone who can understand that by hunting, we are exhibiting and modeling our love, passion, and gratitude for the resource.

And maybe later, in some other offering, I’ll tell you about the wolf.

A Man You Never Knew

Word has reached me, carried on the wind, that Bruno Selmi, legendary owner of Bruno's Country Club, in Gerlach, Nevada, has passed on. I had known that Bruno wasn't feeling well—after stopping in for a visit last year—but am forced to admit that I was nursing a strong and stupid hope that he might live on forever.

Some eras in our lives remain so formative, so rich with experience, that our subconscious keeps them in a special place, preserved in a kind of memorial amber. Bruno, and his watering hole, featured prominently in the personal amber rooms for many of us who once called the great Nevada Outback our home.

Bruno was an immigrant, arriving in Nevada in the 1950s without much English. He bought the Country Club, in those days called the

Longhorn Saloon, for a few thousand bucks. Ultimately, he would own most of Gerlach, build the only motel for a hundred miles in any direction, and become the de facto mayor of a town that never had one. He was a kind of outback Al Swearengen, without the Shakespearean diatribes. Rather, he was acerbic, and possessed a razor wit, which he could, and would, occasionally unleash.

He was a man you could never really know.

The truth is, Bruno never said much at all. He either liked you or he didn't, and if he didn't he would tell you—and he meant it—to get out of his place and go across the street. Only an idiot would ask what was across the street, because the answer was quite clear: nothing but whistling desert.

If less is more, and it often is, Bruno's quiet and laconic nature helped build him into the giant he was, and it may be the reason he was so universally respected, even by those who faced his ire. Because at the bottom of all that ire was a generous heart. He was the kind of guy who would advance a man's paycheck from his own till.

When the first Burners started coming into Bruno's—before Burning Man became the over-hyped and strangely corporatized art-funk techno blowout it is now—they were as nervous and shifty as any troop of dandies stranded at a frontier trading post.

Bruno didn't like them, once warning a man wearing a skirt, and with a hockey puck stuck in his lower lip, that he should be careful walking around the desert because the bird he had wired to the top of his hat was a game species. I only know that is true because I was there when it happened, saw the fear in the poor man's eyes, and heard the bar break up in laughter. But I also know that Bruno eventually came to like them—certainly he liked the money that came with them.

What made Bruno's such a great place wasn't just his stuffed raviolis on a cold day, or the generous drinks he poured. It was the abiding sense, compounded by all of that open desert, that we truly were on a lost frontier, and that the world outside still held the promise of rugged exploration and wild discovery.

The cast of players who inhabited the Country Club on a Saturday night only reinforced the notion. Miners, cowboys, truckers, hunters, itinerant singers, Indians, Mexicans, Whites and Basques, we were all drawn to Bruno's in a kind of marvelous modern rendezvous. It could, and sometimes did, get rowdy.

But the world is always shrinking, slouching toward a kind of sad and somnambulant uniformity, and I think that's a large part of the reason I hold memories of the Country Club, and of Bruno—the master of ceremonies—so dear. His death is, in many ways, the last door on the wild frontiers of my youth slamming shut. Even as things have changed in the intervening decades, his continued life held that door open for a very long time.

I can foresee a day, maybe not long from now, when I will return to the Country Club, belly up to the bar, and order a drink from a sassy bartender with pink yo-yos stuck in his ears. He won't care about anything I might have to say, any stories I might tell of another life, because he was never there to see just how Western the Country Club could be on a Saturday night. He would never have seen Bruno pull out his shotgun to restore order.

And I can imagine my instinctive reaction to the new guy's attitude—the strongest urge to give him an Augustus-McRae-style pistol-whipping.

But I probably won't.

We've graduated from pistol-whipping surly bartenders, it seems. Instead, I'll probably just shrug, stare at my own reflection in the mirror, and pull at a mournfully weak bourbon and seven. And at some point I'll no doubt rally, and raise a quiet toast to Bruno Selmi, and all the other ghosts of yet another lost frontier.

Daybook Entry, 10 September 2018
Figure 8 Ranch

The world is too much with us; late and soon,
Getting and spending, we lay waste our powers;
Little we see in Nature that is ours;
We have given our hearts away, a sordid boon!
This Sea that bares her bosom to the moon;
The winds that will be howling at all hours,
And are up-gathered now like sleeping flowers;
For this, for everything, we are out of tune;
It moves us not. Great God! I'd rather be
A Pagan suckled in a creed outworn;
So might I, standing on this pleasant lea,
Have glimpses that would make me less forlorn;

Have sight of Proteus rising from the sea;
Or hear old Triton blow his wreathèd horn.

—Wordsworth

I often return to the poets these days. From great translations of the *Iliad* and the *Odyssey* to *Beowulf*, from Shakespeare to Dylan Thomas, and more frequently to the modern giants like Charles Wright, Richard Hugo, or Galway Kinnell. I find a touchstone in their visions that gentles my nerves. That ritual works for me because fine poets fire the language with precision, and stoke the imagination with what John Keats called "Negative Capability." The world we inhabit is sorely lacking in appreciation for the mysterious or the levitating, and the airwaves are so rich with insincerity, so overcooked with political certainty and righteous declarations, that the daily and endless caterwauling amounts to a kind of relentless propaganda bullhorn.

They have no poetry at all.

The world is too much with me. It isn't the getting and spending so much, although there is always that. Rather, I've succumbed to a powerful notion that that the body of our republic is diseased, wracked with a stage four cancer, and I am more or less convinced that all of the king's horses and all of the king's men will never quite be able to put her back together again.

It's possible that's just a morose mental conceit in a moment of weakness. Maybe Big America has just always been packed full of angry yahoos flogging their donkeys to death. But every single time I look at social media, or the news—or what passes for news—and increasingly the movies and even the printed press, I come away feeling used and used up, as though I've been sucked into a kind of human-trafficking nightmare where nothing I say, or do, or think, will help me avoid the fate of being repeatedly abused in a kind of digital backwater brothel. After a few minutes of looking or listening, just about all that's left to do is to have my ignorant victimized corpse thrown into a landfill à la Cormac McCarthy's excellent screenplay "The Counselor."

This isn't a new complaint. I once told Allen Ginsberg the same thing over a fruit basket. He pointed out that the problem with television is that you can't talk back to it. This was a long time ago, and Ginsberg, the genius author of "Howl," and other fine poems, had been giving me the glad-eye all night before asking me to stay over. It was raining. We'd already talked about Kerouac and Neal Cassady while Ginsberg ransacked the cupboards for utensils, so I passed on the offer because we'd covered everything I was interested in.

At any rate, that summation of the public conversation—and far too many private ones—is as honest as I can write it. Suffice it to say my tolerance levels for the brazen manipulation of information, and for the moral, political, and spiritual dishonesty on display nearly everywhere I turn, are nearing all-time lows. I find that's true across the board, by the way, regardless of the mouthpiece, the platform, or the means of delivery. There are just far too many opinions jamming up the air, and far too many expectations that we should all share them. And that covers just about every topic I can think of, from paddleboarding to waterboarding.

The last time I hit such a low level of tolerance I jumped out of grad school early and hired on to the 10X Ranch near Twin Arrows, Arizona. I did that after telling the faculty graduate-student advisor that I was giving my students their finals early, and the University could just drop my diploma in the mail. That didn't go over well with Geoffrey, a diminutive east-coast fraternity tart who ran his silo like a re-education camp. In reality, Geoffrey of Dartmouth was little more than a Soviet-style political officer, but my diploma finally reached me on the 3 Dot Ranch in northeastern California, in a battered and torn manila envelope, many moons and many forwarding addresses later.

The 10X was a grand old dame that stretched from the edge of Meteor Crater up into the Mogollons, just south of I-40 heading into Flagstaff. It was full of arrowheads and broken pottery shards come-alive with paint applied by some Navajo woman in the way-far gone. I lived in a shack in the mountains alone and rode herd for a barbed-wire, lunatic ranch manager from Newcastle, Wyoming, named Lee Morris. Lee was old then and I imagine he's dead now. He loved Arizona and hated Wyoming. He said he'd never go back because he was raised taking cold baths in a wooden tub, and after riding with Lee I can only imagine something terrible happened to his child's mind in that country.

Lately, I find myself spending whole days at this computer, trying to crank out some paragraph or a few pages that conjure up some kind of revelatory moment—mostly for myself, but also for the reader—and I'm frequently T-boned in that effort by a hard desire to drop the whole damn enterprise, go outside, saddle the colt, and work on his lateral flexion in a hackamore. It just makes more sense.

Because, really, what solutions do I have for any of these intractable, exceedingly complex, and apparently irreversible problems of modern civilization? How deep into the goo do I really want to wade for some nugget of insight I can easily find jumping out at me from ancient poetry? Poets wearing animal skins and wolf headdresses have already done that work, and the farther we travel along the human timeline, complaints and anxieties don't seem to change very much. Locke and Rousseau were on opposite ends of the modern political spectrum three hundred years ago. So what good is it doing me to read the latest WaPo revelation that General Kelly is shaving his eyebrows off in the West Wing? How is poring over the record of the lies that humanity tells itself, and reinforces by the pundit-pumped gigabyte, helping me do, or think, anything valuable at all?

Having horses around is helpful. I ride at least one of them every day. Mostly I'm focused on the colt. When he and I are done working on simple things in the arena I like to open the gate and ride him outside into the world, stacking important miles and experience on his mind and body before the big winter freeze-up. Out there, in the woods and the canyons and on the scabflats, it's just me on a horse, riding him close and a little firm—he's still a colt after all—and watching the brush for deer we might ride up out of their beds, while wondering just when Big America will find our secret patch of ground and stack a pile of condominiums on it. It does, after all, have some fine canyon and mountain views.

The world is too much with me.

Riding a horse outside often just feels so much more productive than hacking out some trite little column for the local paper, or slaving in service to a novel, because we aren't trying to persuade anybody of anything. We aren't calling out the various historical patterns of doom the nation is falling into, or trying to bring peace to the valley on the topic of wolves, or trying make a joke that can't possibly offend anyone on earth, or worrying about what brand of shoes we aren't supposed to wear. We don't give a loblolly fuck about NAFTA, NATO, or OSHA.

Instead, we think about repetitions, about working for the right feel as a team, about what signals travel down the reins or through my legs that cue him to understand what I'm asking for. We worry about building a relationship on a bedrock of trust, a relationship that by some miracle draws together two wildly different species—predator and prey animal—and makes us into something magnificent, something wholly reduced when one of us is missing.

Out there in the trees and the brush, it's just Remington and cranky old Cowboy Copas—veteran, broncbuster, and steely eyed detective—riding a great saddle built with painstaking perfection on a Wade tree by a saddle-making genius named Matt Plumlee in Eureka, Nevada.

Out there it's just us kids, and we get the wind, and the sun, and the mountains looking down on our trail. We get the birds and the coyotes. We get a long conversation with each other without ever saying a word. And sometimes I sing to him. I sing just loud enough that his ears flicker and I know that he's listening. And I also happen to know that he likes the songs and the way I sing them.

That kind of living is a closed and quiet loop and it feels just right, every damn time, because at the end of the day I can stand with my foot up on the rail of the corral watching him eat and feel dead-centered and rooted directly into the earth's core. I feel balanced and strong as an ox. When we've had a good ride together, and I stand watching him roll in the dust, you couldn't knock me over with a bulldozer.

Try me.

I used to carry my cell phone. I told myself I was doing it in case there was some emergency with my wife, or my daughter, or my uncle; or in case I get tossed into the rocks and break a leg. But really, I brought it to take pictures and share them with the world because I like to brag about this young horse. But I've stopped doing that. For one thing, nobody cares. For another, I've stopped because carrying that obnoxious little slab of circuitry into the holy of holies seems like a violation of something I've been entrusted with. The point is, in case I'm not making it well, I really don't want to "lay waste" my powers out there. I don't want to haul the madding world around in my shirtpocket. If nothing else, Remi deserves a lot more from me.

And if there is some emergency, heaven forbid, well then, by God, people better figure it out.

The ugly truth is, I want the world to bugger-off while I'm building dignity back into my own life, and trying to pour some dignity into the life of a great young horse. I care more about that horse, and how he turns out, than I will ever care about the wild rantings of some sold-out representative in our retail Congress.

Charles Wright, in "Stone Canyon Nocturne," wrote: "No one believes in his own life anymore." I fear he's right about that in a lot of ways, and there is plenty of evidence to support the theory. But we do, on the flipside, seem to have an awful lot of beliefs as they concern other people's lives. And I'm really, really, just very tired of all that. I don't know how, or even if we should, save the planet. I don't have any answers for anyone else on overpopulation, pollution, racial bigotry, or just plain stupidity. I don't have a vision that's going to handle violent crime or illegal immigration. I don't know if Trump is rampaging around the White House with his feet stuffed into knee-boots full of Vaseline, or if the boardroom of the *New York Times* looks like the back room of the Second All-Russian Congress in 1917. Increasingly, I don't even care. Because the truth is I am living so far downstream from all of that horseshit, both physically and mentally, and it is so utterly alien to my daily life, that having an opinion on it is like having an opinion on what's happening on the backside of Saturn. How in the utter fuck can I know what's going on there? And why should I take your word for it?

The truth is, I barely have any answers to explain my own little footprint on the planet, and after a couple of strong pulls off a bottle of Maker's Mark on the porch, on a fine fall evening, I find that even those opinions are surprisingly flexible.

I sometimes wonder what happened to the guy who wrote, in his Daybook on 2 December, 1995, this:

> *"Soldier Meadows Ranch, Nevada. Up early this morning to gather horses. Trailered north and west to Badger Mountain and found seven cows, five calves, one bull sneaking through the sage. Herded them ten miles to the Williams and then rode back to the truck. Very cold all day but no rain; wore my horse down pretty good. It's good country up in there, a lot of feed and good water. I found the cows just west of the Sheldon, but I sure didn't see any wildlife in there. Wonder what causes that. When I got back to the truck I had two flats, so I changed them as the sun set, my feet about to freeze off. Made it back to the ranch well after dark, where I learned that Jerry was rolling his bed. I guess he found a better job elsewhere. That leaves me here alone again. There are still four head up at Badger, and I will go get them tomorrow. Couldn't get around them today. Nearly killed the horse as it was. All look to be dry angus-cross cattle. Some tourists passing through from Reno tonight, riding motorbikes on the desert. Obnoxious children. Weather cold, not too windy. Radio says rain in San Francisco which means snow when it lands here. Too tired to write much more."*

I like that guy a lot more than the jaded and cynical hunchback I'm evolving into. That guy had a different and, I think, better set of priorities. His mind was clear because the inputs were clear. It was simply a question of doing what needed to be done. And there was joy in it. Opinions were virtually useless, and that shows up in the writing. Moreover, the well of that kid's heart was full because there weren't too many buckets trying to draw from it. And I know that I need him back in my life even as I know we can never really close the circle once it's broken.

I need the revenant of that young buckaroo back in my life as much as I need the poems I return to like some medieval penitent whenever I feel the walls closing in. It's true that I am a child of this republic, and so I'm split the way many Americans are split. We are full of manias and violence and insane lusts and sometimes, despite our nature, we manage profound acts of kindness and love and commitment to things bigger than ourselves. I think we are more likely to find Negative Capability in that latter space, but it's fleeting. We hold it in our hands for just a moment and then it dissolves.

In some way, all of this reminds me of my granddad's outlook. He was a hard-bitten son of the Ozarks who joined the Marines to fight Japs, somehow survived, and then spent the rest of his life as a working cowboy. He'd tell me, when I showed up on the ranch wearing existential angst like a bumblebee costume: "Go tug on your balls, Copas." That's one-half of America, I think, the older half that built a republic out of undeveloped wilderness, but there is another gift we can rely on too, and it shows up in little blessings like this bit from James Galvin's masterpiece, *The Meadow*:

> *"Virga is when rain falls and fails to reach the earth, beautiful and useless as the vista it elaborates. Most angels aren't allowed to touch the ground. We pray for real rain to save the pasture; when it doesn't come we pray for rain to keep the timber from burning. Dry lightning pokes at the timber's green dress. Almost every summer there's a major forest fire somewhere near. Every year we*

don't disappear in fire we pray our thanks. The summer Lyle died, fires in Yellowstone four hundred miles away smoked us in so we couldn't see the barn from the house. The sun was gone for weeks. It never did rain, though all summer long flotillas of sheepish clouds sailed in and tried to look like rain. They turned dark and sexual. They let down their hair, like brushstrokes on the air, like feathers of water, like the principle it was named for, sublime indifference its gesture, its lovely signature over us."

Today, the wind came up from the north with a little chill on it, and I walked down to the barn to put a ride on Remi. I've just moved him into a hackamore, which is like moving up from an orange belt to a blue belt in karate. I'm pressed now to use every day at my disposal before the snow flies, because hunting season is coming on and the hours of sunlight and warmth are growing precious. I threw him up in an eight-plait hackamore I picked up at Capriola's in Elko, with a mecate hand-twisted for me by an Apache I once rode with and continue to admire. Old Bert Lambert, who was Mescalero, never did sell his saddle. He never moved to town because he never liked paved roads. Last I heard he was up in Idaho, avoiding town altogether. When I knew him, he used up his winters twisting horsehair into mecates, or making raw-hide strings he braided into beautiful using gear—reatas, bosals, and quirts. These days, because I will probably never see him again, I like to think of him in some mountain camp, twisting the ends of his mus-tache with wax next to a two-dog stove, and making useful, wonderful things, deliberately oblivious to whatever the rest of the world thinks it is doing while the snow cakes in the corners of his window.

But the important part of all of this is that the colt did well today. He likes to learn. He has what horsemen call bottom. I need to figure out a few different ways to show him what I'm asking for, and put new things in front of him, but that's the horseman part. That's the blood part. This horse practically begs me to challenge his mind, to be creative in our conversations, and some days I think the horseman he occasionally draws out of my soul can do almost anything with him. He makes me feel a whole lot better than I actually am. And that will be true so long as we both keep learning.

And so maybe we can close the circle after all. Because right now, in some facsimile of that wiry, nail-eating young buckaroo back in the winter of '95, I've had a great long day in the saddle. And right now, at this moment, the rest of the world doesn't even exist. I'm inside with my slippers on, with the dogs at my feet, and two fingers of Stranahan's in a coffee cup beside the keyboard. And I'm just too damn tired to write another word.

Squaw Creek Rambling Blues

I first noted the change of season on a Friday afternoon. We had a wind-driven break in the wildfire smoke, so I saddled the big mare and rode her out through the woods, across the scabflat, and then slowly along the narrow trail above Squaw Creek Canyon. I was mindful of cats on this ride—a mature female lion killed three pet goats on a cattle ranch near us last week—but with the air finally, albeit briefly, clear of smoke, the chance to mount up and ride was simply too much to resist.

The squirrels have been extraordinarily busy out there.

I noted the change again on Saturday morning, when I was down at the barn and a raft of Canada geese came in low above the trees. There is something ancient in the honking of geese, something in those plaintive notes that corkscrews right up my spine because, like the very best of the blues, they offer a passport into old-earth workings. Maybe it's the way the sound carries in the pines. Maybe it's old memories of the eastern Sierra, high-desert flyways of my youth, when I sat in a haystack calling coyotes, mesmerized by the honest chatter of geese as they winged across a fogbound valley.

Saturday morning the geese were headed west, not south, but it was a prelude to the larger southbound flights we will see and hear in the coming weeks. And one of my favorite moments of later fall comes when I am in my study at night and hear geese honking in the cold pitch-darkness. When that happens I put down my book, or my pen, and close my eyes. And for just a moment I go flying with them through the dark.

If there were any doubt that the Cascades are turning toward fall it was settled this morning. This time of year there is a certain cast of light in the sky, a tint of blue that lets us know the earth has tilted, ever so slightly, while we have been distracted by our frenetic summer business. This morning, as I fed the animals and mucked out the stalls, the sky was a bright fall blue—there was a cool thinness in the wind chasing the trees, and a kind of knowing slowness in the eyes of all four horses. It was that look in the horses' eyes, more than anything else, that sealed it. By noon the door had closed and it felt like summer again, but I had already peeked through the threshold, and once you've seen what's in the room it can never be unseen.

There exists, I think, in early fall, a kissing-cousin to the euphoria we all feel when we've been sick and the fever finally breaks. There is that moment when the body and mind surface from illness. It's a great and lifting instant, when we rise out of sickness, feeling suddenly light and lithe, grateful for a return to good health. And when that happens maybe we are even a little ashamed, or maybe we should be, of taking our health for granted.

Fall, to me, and much more than spring—which holds a more determined kind of promise—always has that feel. Perhaps it's because I know that hunting season is close, that days of stalking an animal with a rifle in the woods, of sharing stories of the hunt and feasting on the harvest, are in the offing. Maybe it's old memories of gathering cattle out of the desert at the end of grazing season. Maybe it's more immediate, like the bright red tomatoes waiting to be picked down in the garden.

Maybe it's just looking forward to long cold nights with a great book, a fire in the hearth, and the dogs at my feet.

Whatever it is, it's this time of year, more than any other, that encourages my mind to ramble and wonder what will become of this place. What will it look like here, on this modest ranch in the ponderosas, in two hundred years?

While riding the mare on the trail above Squaw Creek those thoughts consumed me. Down below, the creek was running, there were deer in the canyon meadow, and I kept thinking about Fremont, who passed through here in 1843, on his way south and to an epic of discovery, adventure, and near starvation before his party finally made it down into the Sacramento Valley.

While sitting the horse on the canyon rim, and watching the low, swift waters run around gravel islands in the creekbed, I was also aware that calling it Squaw Creek is now considered offensive—we are meant to call it Whychus Creek, though I resist that nonsense whenever possible. And I was aware of signage tacked to the trees on a stretch of canyon forest announcing new ownership by a conservancy group—an altogether modern layer on the history of the canyon.

It's that layering of history upon history that interests me. I know that our place, the Figure 8 Ranch, has passed through a number of iterations. Within living memory it has been logged, hunted, and quite suddenly developed. My wife and I are largely responsible for the latter. The house was here, and the shop, but we built the barn, the arena, the turnouts, the garden and the greenhouse. We planted the fruit trees and thinned the junipers. We landscaped it and we fenced it.

We made a house into a home in this rarifying pocket of the less-developed West, and we are grateful for the difference that opportunity has made in our lives.

But what will remain of all this two centuries hence?

There seems to be a natural impulse for human beings to leave a mark. The ochre handprints blown on the walls in the deep recesses of Altamira, for instance, or the Hunger Stones of the Elbe River, where one of the stones reads: "Wenn du mich siehst, dann weine": "If you see me, weep." That remarkable stone, which sits in the Elbe near the northern Czech town of Děčín, records years of drought and famine, beginning in 1417.

This summer, in that country, the stone is fully exposed to the sun.

There are little monuments like that all around us—carvings made by desperate pioneers in the Martian beauty of High Rock Canyon in northwest Nevada, in the petroglyphs carved into stones by Paiutes not a mile from my parents' place on Willow Creek, in northeastern California.

I'm drawn to those quiet little outbursts of humanity demanding attention, that impulse to declare with some permanence: "I was here." It is the same impulse, I suppose, that drove my wife and me to put our handprints in the wet concrete when we built our barn. For good measure, we added the paw prints of our dogs, and I scratched in our names and the date with a nail.

But I wonder who, in some distant future, might look down at that and think about us, or do as I do in the face of a petroglyph and try to conjure the mind and presence of the people who spent hours and days scratching a design into granite. It's a demanding ritual, to stand and admire these things, and like most of history our takeaway can never be more accurate than a police artist's sketch. It's a trick of the mind, a template, a rendering, an impression, and letting our minds run with an outline is perhaps the very best we can ever do.

But there is a critical liminal impulse in both the carving and in the study of the carving, which exist as a kind of Greek sphinx proposing riddles we must solve if we are to survive on the road to Thebes.

I'm drawn to the liminal mind, which seeks an awareness of the layering of history, modernity, and the future. We can do excellent work in that space, where we live and breathe and study in the transition between the old religions and the new ones. But mostly we don't, or can't stay there very long. We've been fragmented so violently by modern culture that it is harder than ever to draw a line from Altamira to the Figure 8 Ranch, from the reed sandals discovered at Ft. Rock to Nike headquarters, and from there into some unknown future—though it seems important that we keep trying.

Jonah Goldberg, writing in *Suicide of the West*, proposes this:

> *"We used to layer meaning atop meaning, horizontally, like one sheet of tinted film atop another. Utility and sacredness, habit and ritual, convenience and tradition, metaphor and fact—each lay atop one another, producing a single lens through which we viewed the world. The scientific revolution changed that. We now hold each sheet of film separately and look at the world through it. We have one sheet for religion. Another for business. Yet another for family. ... By separating out the different meanings of our lives, each one seems more diluted, less all-encompassing and fulfilling. We miss the unity of the pre-Enlightenment mind. And so we yearn to restore meaning where it isn't. We yearn to end the division of labor and find ways of life that are 'authentic' and 'holistic.' We attach ourselves to ideologies that promise unity, where we are all part of the same family or tribe. We flock to leaders on the left and the right who promise to tear down walls and end division—but always on our terms. So much of the rhetoric about the evils of money and the 'capitalist system' isn't really about money but about how so much of our lives has been chopped up by this division of psychic and spiritual labor, banishing the ecstasy of the transcendent from our daily lives. This, in short, is the romantic*

> *temper. The romantic wants to pull down the walls of compartmentalized lives and restore a sense of sacred or patriotic unity of meaning and purpose."*

We are all, I think, if we are trying to do this right, something like the Comancheros, who lived a borderland existence between the Comanche Empire and the Spanish, between the old and the new, between the rising and falling fortunes, and who scouted the future carefully as an entirely new breed called Americans came onto the country. They were liminal in a sense I most admire because they had resilience and pluck, great courage and tenacity, and honored the past with a steady and wary eye on their flanks and on their future.

For the Comancheros, threading the needle was a matter of survival in polar climes. And so too, perhaps, it is for us.

The word "sphinx," incidentally—and only because I mentioned the road to Thebes—comes from the old Greek verb "sphingo" meaning to "squeeze" or to "tighten up," and so it's easy to walk that trail down to the word sphincter, which is a thing that tightens for us all when we watch the evening news, or follow the headlines with any sincerity. Those headlines are almost never liminal or transcendent, they are instead like axe blows on a round of seasoned cordwood, splitting our daily life into pieces meant to feed an all-consuming fire.

Which is a thing I resist by paying attention to the change of season, by watching the geese and the squirrels, and by looking long into a horse's eyes. I resist it by riding a big mare out on the country and letting my mind wander through the trees and among the rocks into the canyon below, an exercise that plugs me into history both far and near and, I suspect, a behavior that will still resonate for free men in some distant future when horse-power may make a triumphant return to the fore.

I promised only the rambling blues, but I'll leave you with this, a final sliding note with a nod to Muddy Waters:

A few days ago I checked on the bees. While the earth was tilting on its axis and the wildfires of perpetual drought were burning, while we were about our madding business of keeping the republic, the bees have been sailing on according to their own compass.

I've learned to work with them without the aid of a suit, moving slowly, talking quietly, like a careful and conscientious houseguest. And so, cautiously, I cracked the super with my hive tool. And here was my liminal moment: even before I lifted the inner cover I could smell it, richly aromatic, not wafting so much as flooding my bloodstream by syrupy transfusion—the ancient and eternal gift of glistening, golden, saturating honey.

And as I stood there I suddenly realized that all of it—the bees, the honey, the hive, my earthly body and the grass and the trees, were floating in a cloud of smoke.

Cool Water

Out here in the American West, water is always precious, particularly when living on the east side of any of the hundreds of mountain ranges between the Sierra-Cascades and the Rockies. Out here, the east side of anything is always the drier side, the rainshadow side, and so east-siders live within a perpetual loop of drought and diminishing returns. The diminishing returns are a result of aggressive settlement beyond the 100th Meridian, which is desert, and has been a desert since before the end of the last ice age.

The illusion of abundance in the western deserts was easy enough to sustain for more than a hundred years because the impacts of so many people were spread over hundreds of thousands of square miles. Even the larger hydrology projects such as the draining of the Klamath Basin (which destroyed the Klamath Basin) or the construction of the LA

Aqueduct (which destroyed the Owens Valley) primarily impacted rural areas. In those deeply rural areas—which in both the Klamath and Owens cases also happened to be major stopping points along the Pacific Flyway—the few people living there had no power to prevent what remains the insane vision of settling millions upon millions of people in a desert. A desert that simply cannot sustain the ever-increasing draws on water.

In California, where 25.5 million acres of land are given over to farming in the production of some 400 separate commodities—even as many of those crops and commodities are falling inexorably into the monoculture trap and are owned by hostile foreign entities—the essential water infrastructure has not been updated since the WPA projects of the 1930s. In 1930 there were fewer than six million people living in California. Today there are more than 40 million people, and many millions more that don't show up on a census. Most of those people take showers every day, wash their dishes and clothes, brush their teeth, flush toilets, water their lawns and gardens, wash their cars, irrigate their fields, or use up water in any number of other daily activities. Estimates are that in California the average person uses 71 gallons of water every day. And in parts of the Central Valley, where more than 100,000 unregulated irrigation wells draw daily from 20,000 year-old aquifers, the valley floor has dropped nearly 30 feet.

But breeding even more human beings, settling and developing even more of the desert, continues to be the dominant theme. "Growth" is the only way to sustain the economic model even if the end result is the practical exhaustion of the most important resource required to make the models a reality. The population of California is projected to reach nearly 60 million by 2050, though almost no one seems to be discussing where the water supplies will come from.

This winter—I'm writing this in March of 2019—the Sierra snowpack stands at 136% of normal. It is the fifth highest snowload ever recorded in the Sierras. At Donner Pass between Reno and Sacramento the snow is nearly 30 feet deep. That's great news except that California is unable to capture significant portions of the 580 billion gallons of water that snow represents, because environmental regulations prohibit the building of new dams and reservoirs. This is true even as the collapse of the Oroville Dam last year exposed significant problems in the existing infrastructure. And because they can't capture the water, record snowfalls and atmospheric rivers don't mean as much as they otherwise might. And the unspoken fear is that next year may always be the start of another extended drought, only with more and more people taxing the already limited resource.

Here in Central Oregon—where we live on the east side of the Cascades—and where the geology, ecosystem, and climactic conditions are similar to those of our cousin range in the Sierras to the south—we have been clobbered by a late-February snowstorm. Estimates vary but even here in Sisters, at a mere 3200 feet of elevation, we've received three or more feet of snow. Our reservoirs, from Crane Prairie to Prineville, are now full.

Crane Prairie reservoir has a carrying capacity of more than 55,000 acre-feet of water, and nearby Wickiup (both reservoirs were created by damming the Deschutes River) is capable of carrying some 200,000 acre feet of water. Having those reservoirs full is a celebratory event, but the question for us remains: how can we keep demanding so much of an arbitrary and therefore finite resource?

Central Oregon, with a growth rate reliably over 3.5% annually, is filling up with people, many of them political and economic refugees from the disaster of California. And because we are occasionally enchanted by an abundance of water, we aren't often discussing the most important long-term question: at what point do we reach critical mass?

Oregonians nurture a superior attitude toward most things California, but we don't seem to be learning many of the lessons that California offers, and meaningful distinctions between the two states—from agricultural policies to in-house politics—are diminishing to the point of nonexistence.

Democratic Socialist Alexandria Ocasio-Cortez, the freshman representative for New York's 14th district, has been routinely throat-punched in the media for some of her ill-considered pronouncements, but there are some underlying truths in her crusade for a Green New Deal that we would be foolish to ignore. Because our resources are not infinite, the sooner we wake up to that startling fact the better chance we have to avoid some very painful and potentially disastrous long-term outcomes. Famine and starvation aren't phenomenons limited to East Africa, and while reasonable people can argue endlessly about environmental issues, from fossil fuel exploitation to alternative energy projects, if there isn't enough water to support the people where they want to live, none of those discussions mean anything at all. And that fact alone—the unpredictability of future water resources—opens a Pandora's box of ethical and environmental considerations that so far no one in political power has mustered the temerity to address in a meaningful way.

Except perhaps for Gavin Newsom, the governor of California, who has at least openly mentioned California's "massive water problems," and recently proposed a drinking-water tax in California in order to create a "safe and affordable drinking-water fund" for the southern San Joaquin Valley and the Mojave Desert—where drinking water supplies are contaminated by toxins. Adding industrial agricultural pollution to already scant water supplies is a particularly modern conundrum with no end in sight because there will only ever be more and more people needing food, which requires more water, which isn't easy to provide in a desert. And, like most other things in California, their first and only solution to the problem is a tax that likely won't solve any problems at all.

Which is one reason the growth mavens are now looking to tap the Cadiz Aquifer in the Mojave Desert. As the *Washington Post* reported earlier this month: "The aquifer is roughly the size of Rhode Island. Cadiz would draw water from the ground, pump it east through a proposed 43-mile pipeline to the Colorado River Aqueduct, then sell it to water districts as far as 200 miles away. An estimated 100,000 households could be customers during the project's initial 50-year term, which would generate billions of dollars in revenue for the company."

But the problem from drawing water from aquifers—including the Cadiz which is also federally protected land—is that in many cases it took 10-15,000 years for those aquifers to be created in the first place. What is the long-term proposal to recharge them in the age of climate change? Watering 100,000 households on the resource for an initial 50-year term may sound appealing on the surface, but what about year 51? Should we just continue ducking any responsibility and let our grandkids sort that out, or is the search for water like the search for oil, an endless exploration creating short-lived benefits and long-term catastrophe?

Human beings, and Americans in particular, have driven this phenomenon since the end of the First World War, and are remarkably short-sighted about our professed values. If we are to honor community and family and so many of the other tropes wrapped up in hot dogs and Chevrolet and the Stars and Stripes, then we must be smart and bold enough to address some very real questions about how we intend to preserve them in the long run as we continue stacking millions of people into places that won't sustain them.

There are undeniable limitations placed on us by natural planetary facts—which the natives understood in a culturally self-limiting way—that we ignore at our own peril. Our reliance on economic growth as the measuring stick for all things may instead lead to our own utter destruction. Because housing developments built on a fetishistic dream belie the fact that our resources are exquisitely finite. No one can predict how much rain or snow we will get in the next fifty years; and if climate change is real and sustained over time, then large portions of the American West may end up looking more like Timbuktu than the present-day metropolitan wonders of Las Vegas and Los Angeles.

This is a choice we are making.

When my wife and I first married we lived in Lake Almanor, California. She was a student where I was a teacher at Lassen College in nearby Susanville, California. Our home at the lake, nearest an inlet called Hamilton Branch and not far from the small logging town of Chester, California, backed into the forest and was about a quarter mile from the lake. The house we lived in was built by Wendy's great-grandfather, who had made his future in the citrus groves of southern California as an early beneficiary of the LA Aqueduct. He built a successful inland empire in the desert with that water, taking advantage of decent soil and perfect weather. But those groves are all gone now, given over to urban sprawl and gargantuan housing developments that use far more water than the groves ever did.

And even Lake Almanor, which remains remote enough to have avoided some of the major tourist pitfalls of other pristine mountain towns in the northern Sierras, is a fake. Created by the construction of Canyon Dam, the lake occupies a valley once known as Big Meadow, and before that was home to many hundreds of generations of Maidu people who can't even get federal recognition as a tribe despite 10,000 years of living there.

What fascinates me, as I contemplate the desert from my desk—while looking out at three feet of snow—is that some thirty feet below the water of Lake Almanor sits the town of Prattville. Prattville is a quiet favorite among mountain lake divers, a club of hearty souls in the same phylum as cavers, and much like cavers people who see the world with a very different awareness of its history. A good mountain diver can drop into Lake Almanor and fin between the treetops of Big Meadow, or watch the fish swim through windows of the Prattville General Store.

In the modern West we have as many challenges as we do options. We can teach the truth or we can teach fundamental lies that make us all feel better when we're waiting on tenterhooks for the final season of "Game of Thrones." We can choose to embrace certain realities the planet offers us, or we can ignore them. If history is our guide it seems likely we will ignore them. And if we ignore them then we are foolish, but we will at least have our memes, and our conflicts of politics and religion (or the even-more-rabid insistence on no religion at all) and sunshine daydreams about economic growth and ease, and our flimsy notions of a sustainable future. But without enough water—cool, clear, water—we will inevitably share the same drastic future. Whatever our most passionately held beliefs may happen to be.

THE SUMMER OF WOMEN

Here on the Figure 8, it is the summer of women. I admit to difficulties in the transition. For lengthy seasons in this life I have operated altogether outside the influence of women, marooned entirely alone on the desert, for instance, or crammed into warships with a battalion of humorless leathernecks. And if anywhere there truly is a man's world, look no further than the Marine Corps berthing spaces on board Naval Shipping—it is like living in a bobbing jar full of angry hornets.

But this summer my daughter is here. An adult now, she is training and studying for the demands of the hard career she has chosen and, together with my wife they have—either by accident or design—embarked on an aggressive plan for my re-education and reintegration.

I am being "mainstreamed."

Thus far, my faulty grocery-shopping strategies have been corrected. I now understand that the shortest distance between two points is not, after all, a straight line, but rather a meandering, philosophical, ingredient-reading, chatting, backtracking, calorie counting, visiting, and randomly deviating course between the sour cream and the salad dressing.

I have been wrong about that for years.

Also, there are certain things that must never go in the dishwasher, ever, under any circumstances, for reasons that are apparently classified. This is also true of the microwave. And, alarmingly, there are strict procedures and protocols involving various detergents and temperature settings on the washing machine.

In my own defense, I have always done my own laundry. For years I just used shampoo because I couldn't see any reason to buy ten different kinds of soap. I mixed colors and washed everything with warm water. It worked. I have now learned that this was bad behavior.

I think I still have the dogs on my side, but ultimately they are, as well as the colt, eunuchs, which isn't helpful when I try to build a coalition of men to defend my less-considered tendencies.

And it isn't just my wife and daughter who look at me sideways. Elsewhere on the rancho there are two agitated mares, seven attitudinal chickens, and a lunatic barn cat who kills things daily—all of them serving to remind me of Karen Blixen's marvelous line from "Out of Africa": "You know you are truly alive when you are living among lions."

Women, I think, have consistently failed to realize and exploit their full powers. Women stand poised on the very precipice of world domination. It's likely they always have, and even more likely that they already know this. I don't know why they haven't yet taken over—unless it is because they'd just rather not.

Please don't misunderstand me. I haven't simply turned in my man-card and given up. I resist this new wife-daughter axis daily, in guerilla fashion, occasionally and weakly resorting to a rather juvenile kind of muttering under my breath. Which is probably better than caterwauling and throwing fine china at the menials, like Richard Burton on a three-day bender in Saint-Tropez.

Meanwhile, when the women in my life blast off to yoga and I am allowed to peek at the news, I see that the President of the United States continues tweeting like a sixth-grader who just swallowed a lemon, and the entire State of Illinois has been downgraded to junk status.

A strange summer, indeed.

I'm exaggerating all of this, of course. But it does raise a poignant question: what would I do without these lovely women that I love? I have some ideas, none of them good, and most of them involving strange visions of myself wandering aimlessly through the Nevada desert in torn trousers and ratty slippers, looking like a bald, piratical hybrid of Harry Dean Stanton and Edward Abbey.

The truth is, I am enthralled and grateful daily, and despite the corrections—some harsher than others—of my attitudes and behaviors, I am in full admiration and appreciation for the women in my life. While it is true that they occasionally drive me to the slippery edge of total insanity, I wouldn't change a thing.

I feel like the speaker in Jim Wright's poem "A Blessing" who is approached by horses in a spring pasture. Their world, he knows, is entirely their own. "There is no loneliness like theirs," he says, accepting that there are things about them he will never understand. But even across that gulf, they have walked over and welcomed him as a guest, and he longs most to be amongst them.

He stands admiring the horses for the longest time and then, suddenly, realizes that his love for them is so encompassing, so joyful, so powerful, that "if I stepped out of my body I would break into blossom."

And so it is these warm summer evenings, with the dogs napping and shadows stretching across the grass, when we gather on the porch to unwind the day and find each other again, that I listen to my wife and daughter quietly talking and laughing, and watch them when they don't know it, and feel every cell in my body beginning to bloom.

Ed O'Farrell's Midnight Ride

On a recent research trip into the Nevada outback, *Nugget Newspaper* editor Jim Cornelius and I had occasion to stop for a few minutes in Silver Lake, Oregon—to pay our respects at a monument in the local cemetery. Ten feet high, unprepossessing, the monument was erected in 1898, to remember the victims of Oregon's most deadly fire.

The Silver Lake fire of 1894 isn't really the stuff of a Christmas column, except that in the midst of an agonizing tragedy there were also towering acts of selflessness.

For the two hundred or so people who gathered in the J.H. Clayton Hall—a community room built above Chrisman Brothers Mercantile—it was a chance to get out of the minus-twenty-degree cold. It was also Christmas Eve, and after weeks of anticipation, finally time to celebrate the Christmas Tree Program with family and friends who had come in buggies, wagons, and on horseback, from ranches and homesteads as far away as Paisley.

Silver Lake was then not much bigger than it is now, and in 1894 it was the only established trading post between Prineville and Lakeview.

The community hall, which had been used for dances, theater programs, and the occasional foot-stomping lecture by wandering evangelists, was decorated with a large Christmas tree. The tree was piled up with presents, and the walls were decorated with paper chains and pine branches. At one end of the hall there was a small stage for the choir, and the guests were seated, shoulder-to-shoulder, on an assortment of planks, benches, boxes, and the occasional chair.

The celebration was almost at an end, the choir wrapping up its last song of the night, when George Payne, eighteen, stood up from his seat and tried navigating through the crowd by walking along the edge of a bench. Focused on keeping his balance, George cracked his head on a Rochester lamp hung from the ceiling, "causing it to slosh coal oil into the burner and flare and flame inside."

The inferno that followed would cost the lives of forty-three people.

There were plenty of heroic efforts among the general panic that night. There was Francis Chrisman, who grabbed the burning lamp with his bare hands. It was a heroic move that ended poorly when people began batting at the fireball, causing Chrisman to drop the lantern—where it was kicked away in the stampede. Burning oil then spread in all directions, and caught a young woman's dress on fire.

There was Walter Duncan, who climbed out onto the porch roof and handed some twenty people down into the street and safety. And there was John Buick, who carried his infant daughter and young son Frank, through the flames.

For many, there was no way out at all. Built above the mercantile, the Clayton Hall had only one exit, at the bottom of a narrow corridor, with a door that opened into the crowd that was now pressing down the stairs. But for Lucinda Schroeder, who had initially escaped the fire and who returned to search for her husband and son, nearly a hundred more people may have died. She stood blocking the door open with her body so that others could escape.

Both Schroeder and her son would perish in the flames.

After George Payne's head struck the lamp it took only two minutes for the entire building to go up in flames. Outside, "water was pumped on those stumbling out of the building with their clothes aflame, until the hose rig jammed. Then the stairs, heavy with people, collapsed."

And there was Ed O'Farrell, a young buckaroo, who climbed on his horse and set out across the desert, in the middle of the night, to fetch the closest doctor. Anyone who has done any serious riding in that kind of cold, at night, can appreciate the magnitude of this feat, and we are left to wonder what he might have been thinking as he started out into the miles of snow and ice with an inferno raging in the winter darkness over his shoulder.

The physician, a Dr. Bernard Daly, was in Lakeview, a hundred miles away.

But O'Farrell rode through, changing horses at ranches along the way, and arranging a relay of fresh mounts for the return trip. He finally arrived in Lakeview on the afternoon of Christmas day, some fifteen hours after setting out.

When Dr. Daly arrived in Silver Lake, early on December 26th, "every house in the village had been turned into a hospital." Among the dead were nineteen women and eight children. For days afterward, citizens of the Oregon outback continued to arrive in Silver Lake, to lend whatever hand they could in the wake of unimaginable horrors.

The monument in Silver Lake is a grim, grey thing. And it was a grim, grey day when Jim and I parked on the side of the road to explore and behold it. And as we set out again, heading east into even deeper reaches of desert history, I could not stop thinking about Ed O'Farrell.

I could not stop hearing the creak of cold saddle leather as he rode, or stop feeling the bitter, burning frost in his fingers and toes. I could not stop hearing his horse, laboring to punch through mile after mile of crusted snow and ice. And I could not stop admiring the size of a man's heart who would continue in that way, long after the warm and terrible fire glow had been subsumed, when even time finally froze solid and night rushed into the void like the hardest dark.

Black Rock Blues

I admit to a conservative streak in my nature. One problem with that is a tendency to paint the past in golden hues and promote a world that never really existed. And it's probably accurate that if we are ever to learn anything and carry that knowledge forward, we can't do it by living too long in the rearview mirror.

This was brought home to me recently on a visit to Bruno's Country Club, in Gerlach, Nevada. I was by turns outraged and appalled to find it had undergone severe modernization. Honestly, the end result was a wholesale ransacking of memories I've cherished for a very long time.

There were still some deer and antelope mounts on the wall. There was a faded picture of Scottish speed freak Richard Noble, looking admirably composed after surviving a six-hundred-thirty-three-mph jet-car ride across the Black Rock playa. And there was still a dusty old pheasant flushing forever beside the new digital jukebox.

But the frontier flavor of Bruno's was erased, replaced by an absurdly modern bar—a kind of characterless theater in the round, adorned with flat screen televisions and ergonomic barstools, and worse—a faux granite bartop that released a sickening odor of scented bleach.

That was new, too. Bruno's idea of cleaning the bar was rubbing his shirtsleeve down the length of it, which somehow defeated dangerous microbes for about forty years.

But Bruno is gone now and the remodel, I suspect, was an effort to appeal to the start-up unicorns and ecstasy executives who've turned the yearly Burning Man party into a grinding expression of self-indulgence tailor-made for YouTube.

Those modernist types have a problem too, it turns out, which is opposite of the one I have: they don't seem to appreciate anything that is more than ten minutes old.

Don't get me wrong. I root for hippies, or hipsters, or whatever reluctant capitalists are called when they grow beards and man-buns and adopt that snarky millennial je ne sais quois—but who nevertheless can't quite change a tire, scramble an egg, or find Kansas on a map.

I really do root for them, because dancing around a dry lakebed with hockey pucks in their earlobes is probably, in the end, an inexpensive vote for humanity and our shared karma. And, no doubt, the world needs more angry middle-class white kids in dreadlocks and denouncing privilege while praising the divine rights of Haile Selassie and chortling artisanal bongs in a Nevada sandstorm.

And certainly—I can't resist—no lasting harm is done when a gentrified baby boomer tries to rediscover his glory years by fabricating a street-legal steam calliope, and then drives it from Portland to Gerlach with a backseat full of vaping tattoo artists and a jockey box stuffed with Viagra.

I root for them because it's clear to me that we need these people now more than ever. Especially after the city of Chicago managed to clock out of 2017 with only six hundred fifty murders, which is perhaps an encouraging sign that meditation gardens and Saturday drum circles are finally having an impact on world peace.

But did they have to destroy the last good cowboy bar for a hundred and fifty miles in any direction?

I wonder this in light of Kerouac's aging but accurate diagnosis of so much that is wrong with humanity—which is the collectively desperate effort to appear cosmopolitan.

Granted, I was in a bad mood when we finally made it to Bruno's. That mood was born far out on the desert, around midnight, with the noisy braying of wild burros—mean spirited little animals who wrecked a perfectly good dream featuring Raquel Welch in a deer-hide bikini.

And, soon after, my companion and I were treated to a deluge of wind and freezing rain that drove us out of our bedrolls and into the cab of my truck, where we sat like pickled vagrants for six hours, listening to Burl Ives sing "Go Tell Aunt Rhody" on an endless loop.

We were only sixty miles of washboard road from Bruno's, but I remained optimistic. In the morning we had planned to scout Little High Rock Canyon, where Shoshone Mike and the last free natives killed four sheepherders in 1911. Like Bruno's, that canyon is part of my own history in the region, but I'd forgotten how fast the weather can turn, and snow had ruined the prospect.

So, at sunrise, our camp wrecked, our gear soaking and scattered across the desert, we passed on desert history, conceded defeat to the elements, and headed for the luxuries of town, where the rude discovery of the Country Club's makeover awaited.

But even with its defeats, a trip like that can never be counted a loss.

Two nights earlier we had made our camp high above Summit Lake, in a grove of quaking aspens cut through by Mahogany Creek. We ate like kings around a good campfire and slept soundly. There was an old line-shack near our camp, a sad and gutted thing leaning over in time, harried by the elements. I had known that shack in its prime, long before it fell into disuse.

But the shack was still there, and looking back now, I realize that in its own way, that old cow camp was both a warning about what we would eventually find at Bruno's, and an excellent reminder about living too hard in the past. It reminded me that nothing ever stays the same, and that the gift of grace is perhaps best realized when we honor all that has gone before. Which is a thing we do best by learning to embrace the future all of that history made possible.

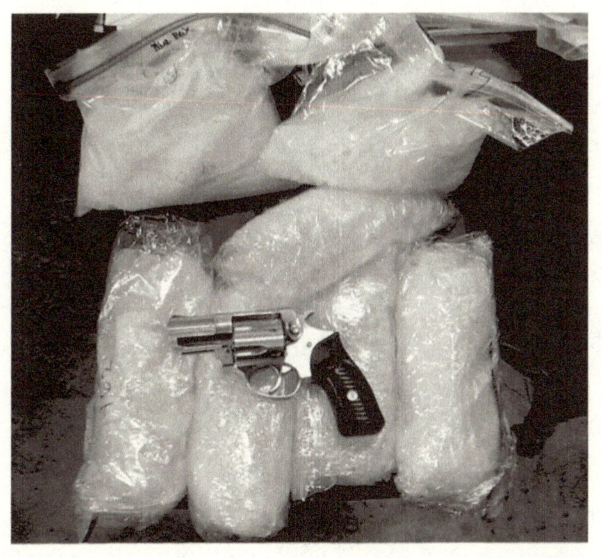

The People I Didn't Kill

The soul of a cop's eyes
Is an eternity of Sunday daybreak in the suburbs
Of Juárez, Mexico.

— James Wright, "The Minneapolis Poem"

Yesterday, after a luxurious week of toiling underground, minding my own business, breaking the code of a hard poem by Rilke, sitting on the porch to watch the hawk who was watching our chickens, shooting twice—and missing—at the coyote who slinks in from the trees to salivate at the henhouse door, I made a tragic mistake: I came up for air.

The air, it turns out, is bad, full of Ferguson, Missouri, and smoke from that fire. Two minutes of television news: shrieking and hand-wringing, nabob commentary, industrial shouting matches. That's it, that's all there was.

Television journalists have done more than kill the ghost of Walter Cronkite, they have become tenured professors in the Jerry Springer School of Commentary and Analysis, stoking the generational embrace of identity politics and grievance theater.

It made me want a drink. A hard rye whisky. Neat. Instead, I strapped on my Asics and went for a run in the woods, always a better choice, and was rewarded for that rare moment of discipline. The woods were quiet and warm, the treetops in full sun. There was only the sound of my feet on the trail, the birds and the small creatures alarming as I ran by, and my own labored breathing on a steep, rocky hill.

Recently I was asked how many people I killed when I was a cop. It wasn't the first time. Like doctors forced to diagnose illness at every cocktail party, cops (and former cops) endure a battery of complaints about law enforcement at every turn. No couples' dinner is safe. A roadside chat with a friendly neighbor quickly devolves into a conspiracy rant against their recent speeding ticket, and by extension, naturally, the militarization of law enforcement, blue helmets, and black helicopters. Cops accept this, like vomit in the back of a squad car, idiot lieutenants, and late-night alley fights with psychotic tweakers, because it comes with the territory.

Sadly, the inevitable harangue almost always reveals too much about the person giving it.

In this case the question came from a young person, and they can be forgiven the crudity of their curiosity, even if it is backloaded with tired assumptions force-fed by bad television, video games, abysmal schools, and that grandest of American traditions: the full criminal embrace. While the characterization of cops has migrated from the Officer Friendly types on Adam 12 to masked bogeymen in "tanks" fiendishly no-knocking the wrong house, outlaws and very bad people enjoy the fruits of selective judgment.

We still love Jesse James. Charles Manson married his pen pal. Bernie Madoff's underwear sold at auction for two hundred dollars.

But the *question* was wrong. As I ran through the woods, following the trail where it wound through a dry creek, I thought about the people I didn't kill.

I didn't kill Gary T., Jr., a career criminal and dimwit who pointed a loaded crossbow at me and my partners (after he ran inside his house and barricaded himself in the upstairs bedroom). I could have, but I didn't. I also didn't kill Eddie V.T., a disturbed Iraq war veteran, on the La Cumbre overpass, though I held his solar plexus squarely in the crosshairs of my rifle while he brandished a handgun at me and my partners—an incident broadcast live on CNN. I didn't kill Manuel B., late one night when he was sawing through the backdoor of his girlfriend's house, smoked out of his mind on meth, intending to *kill her*; he settled for attacking my partner and me with a live reciprocating saw. I didn't kill Jose R., because he was too fast, I was too slow, and the man he'd just shot four times in the parking lot was bleeding out in my arms.

I might have killed all of these people, but I didn't.

I have a good friend who reminded me once, while we shared a coffee between calls for service, our backs to the wall in an alcove on the urine-soaked and bum-stinking low-rent side of the Monopoly board, that it has only been in the last hundred years or so that good people have been forced to tolerate criminals. Not so very long ago, but in another world altogether, it seems a gentleman might run a bandit through with a sword. And decent people were decently grateful. In modern America, that same gentleman is not only forced to tolerate the bandit, but must also give him a job. In other words, the modern American gentleman must, by law, help the bandit rob the other passengers on the coach.

We've come a long way indeed.

I don't know what happened in Ferguson. Nobody else does either. One of the actors is dead, the other might as well be, and eyewitnesses are notoriously unreliable. Still, the fires keep burning, a failed and suspect POTUS keeps popping off between rounds of golf, and the race hustlers have flown in on their private jets.

But I know this much: if the young officer who fired his weapon did wrong, he will pay the price. He is already paying the price. And here's the rub for those good people charged with the thankless task of policing this nation: it is likely that *even if he did nothing wrong at all*, legally, morally, or otherwise, he will be sacrificed, like the sloe-eyed lamb, on the altar of race relations—if only to stop the looting of spinner rims from Auto Zone.

And tonight, while America sleeps off another heavy meal of sensationalist journalism, hardworking police officers will face tens of thousands of dangerous situations without killing anyone—though they might have, and no one will offer so much as a cursory "thank you" in the morning.

In the meantime, smoke from our own wildfires is casting an orange pall on the ponderosas. Harry Dean Stanton, the ranch cat, is stalking chipmunks down by the greenhouse, the dogs are asleep on the back porch, and the chickens gave us four eggs this morning. The coyote, perhaps leery of another bullet creasing his forehead, is somewhere else in the forest. The hawk is still in his tree, because he is hard-eyed royalty. But he is always there, and I'm going for another run.

The Anti-Millennial

Perhaps you've seen them, those strange millennials, that generation of young and loud Americans best known for Pajama Boy memes and Justin Bieber, a mincing bunch in need of safe spaces and trigger warnings, who may not know where their food comes from but voice strong opinions about everything from climate change to global trade initiatives.

Perhaps, at the end of a hard day's work, you've seen all of that on the evening news and felt some rising level of despair for our shared future.

But there is a strong case for hope. It exists firmly in young ranchers like Jesse Midgely, twenty-four, of Janesville, California, who isn't just breaking the millennial mold, but is shattering the popular perception of youth from any age. Jesse is only one man, but he represents thousands of young American farmers and ranchers quietly toiling in flyover country, young men and women who rarely show up in commercial media, who have inherited a legacy of hard work, commitment to a family ranch, and service to a purpose larger than themselves.

Midgely was raised by his grandparents in northeastern California's Honey Lake Valley, in the shadow of the northern Sierras. His grandfather, David Pingree, was born in a canvas tent on a ranch near McDermitt, Nevada, and his grandmother Glennys came into the great basin from the Reeves Ranch, near Granola, Kansas. David and Glennys met at a farmhouse party in Johnstonville, were married, and settled on Sears Road, in the heart of Lassen County's hay and cattle country.

Jesse credits his grandparents for the drive he needs to raise seventy-five pairs and hay two hundred acres, all while holding down a full-time job at the Diamond Saw Shop in Susanville.

"The worst thing you could say was that you were bored," Jesse says of his childhood, "Or Grandpa was going to put you to work. The punishment for being bored was to clean out the stock trailer with a square-tip shovel. You couldn't just sit around. When my friends came over, we couldn't be inside. We had to be outside doing something. If he saw us just sitting around he'd bring out the boxing gloves, and pretty soon we'd be boxing."

But Jesse's grandfather, a Navy veteran of the Korean War, wasn't all work. "He was also patient," Jesse says. "He would make the time for fun. We did a lot of hunting and fishing."

Jesse's grandmother worked as a teacher's aide and cafeteria hand at Shaffer School, in nearby Litchfield. "Grandma was really active," Jesse says. "She was pretty tough, persistent, always asking me if I was doing this or that, and if not, wanting to know why it wasn't getting done."

When he was fourteen, Jesse's grandfather took him aside and gave him the proposition that charted the course of his life. "Listen," Jesse recalls him saying, "If you want to keep this ranch going, you can, but you have to make a decision." While other kids his age were fighting over playing time on XBox, Jesse committed himself to carrying on his family legacy, and has never looked back.

At Lassen High School, in Susanville, Jesse was involved with FFA, raising steers, completing welding projects, and "dirt-judging," as he calls it. After high school, he attended Lassen College, where he studied agriculture science and earned his certificates in welding.

Jesse's impressive and decidedly anti-millennial schedule can be a relentless grind, and he isn't always able to go along when his friends invite him out for a time on the town, but he says "I weigh it all out, and I still think it's worth it. At the end of the day you can look back and see that you accomplished something."

During haying season Jesse is up each morning and on the tractor from three thirty in the morning until seven thirty, when he breaks to go to work at the saw shop. After work, he comes back to the ranch and labors until the job is finished, which can easily mean midnight. His weekends are scheduled far in advance. "There is always something I need to do," he says, whether it's moving cows between pastures, fixing fence, or working on one of his three tractors. "Which isn't any fun, by the way," he says with a laugh.

Glennys passed away last year, preceded by David, and Jesse feels the weight of their absence. "Now I gotta use my own brain," he says. "I've got nobody pounding ideas into my head." But he does have occasional help from his girlfriend, Ginger Miller, an Ag Science major at the University of Nevada, and a small cadre of longtime family friends who gather to help with brandings. Jesse appreciates their help, and enjoys "the stories they can tell me about my granddad."

In an age when many of his peers are wallowing in pools of millennial angst, pointing fingers at the world and demanding entitlements, Jesse is working relentlessly, seeking opportunities to improve his ranch and his herd, secure new leases, and expand his ranching horizons.

When asked why, Jesse thinks for a minute and says, "Because I can't stand waste. And because it's fun." He pauses for a moment, thinking, then says with a wink, "And maybe it's because I like to gamble. Maybe that's it."

Despite the challenges, Jesse loves his ranch, and the work. He has a firm grasp of the pressures that attend ranching in the modern West, from the endless parade of new and fruitless government regulations to environmentalist intrusions into private property rights. "You have to like doing it," Jesse says. "You have to care about your legacy, about not letting it die, and in the end, when it's all said and done, it's worth it."

When asked to look into the future, to describe the primary threats to young ranchers looking to succeed, Jesse responds without missing a beat. "Wolves and democrats," he says, with his trademark smile.

This Jump's for You, Chief

"... I can remember everything: From horse and cart days right up until today; jet planes and computers. When I was a boy there weren't even any fences ... all just open prairie. The world has changed so quickly ... It's so short a time ... I've had a long life, but it seems like yesterday ..."

—Chief David William Wounded in Winter Beautiful Bald Eagle

Chief David Beautiful Bald Eagle died on July 22, 2016. He was born in a tipi on the edge of the Cheyenne River on April 8, 1919, and he was the grandson of Chief White Bull, who some 43 years earlier had led a memorable charge against Custer at the Little Bighorn. In 1936 Beautiful Bald Eagle joined the U.S. Army's 4th Cavalry, and in 1940 re-enlisted with the 82nd Airborne at Fort Bragg. He was decorated for bravery after his first combat jump at Anzio; and was severely wounded and left for dead on his second, at Normandy, on D-Day.

After the war, Beautiful Bald Eagle played semi-pro baseball. He acted in movies and served as Errol Flynn's stunt double in *Flaming Arrow*. He became a champion ballroom dancer and is enshrined in the Ballroom Hall of Fame. He raised horses. He raised children—a lot of them: 25 in fact, including five that he and his wife—an actress from Belgium named Josee, whom he met at the World's Fair in 1958—adopted. He raced cars. He went back to rodeo, forking bareback broncs and bulls. He was a close friend of Casey Tibbs, and once danced with Marilyn Monroe. He acted in more movies, including *Dances With Wolves*, and starred in his final film at the age of 95. In the late 1990s he was made traditional Chief of the Minniconjou Lakota, in 2001 was elected first Chief of the United Native Nations, named a Goodwill Ambassador for the Cheyenne River Sioux, and then he went skydiving.

Skydiving.

I've seen a lot of that lately, while working the horses down by the barn or out watering the garden. The Figure 8 is not far from the Sisters Airport, and these days I can often look up and see the brightly patterned canopies swinging slowly back to earth. On some days I can even hear the delighted shrieks and shouts of people living their lives with a dramatically renewed sense of awe.

Surely you know what comes next.

What better way to honor a life of service and dedication to family, friends, neighbors, a life so well lived, so perfectly bookended by tipis and super-computers, that it almost defies articulation? Why wouldn't we, after considering one man's model, take a minute to examine the mundane routines that we fall into so easily, throw them out with Monday's garbage, and purposefully aim for a place completely beyond our comfort zone?

So Wendy and I decided to do it. We decided to fall the through the sky together as a means to honor the Chief, and to plug ourselves back into that side of life that still carries an electric charge.

It wasn't hard to do. We just jumped in the truck and drove down to the airport to sign up, entrusting our lives to a pair of complete strangers. Ryan and Steven, with something like ten thousand skydives between them, gave us a half-minute or so of confident instruction and then packed us into the surprisingly simple uniform of human flight: harness and jumpsuit. And it was not lost on me—as we flew over the drop zone and Ryan cinched up our tandem rig so tight I could barely feel my toes—that Beautiful Bald Eagle believed that the harness he wore on D-Day had saved his life, as he and his brothers from the 82nd were shot, "like clay pigeons" descending over Normandy. The harness was so tight, Beautiful Bald Eagle said, that it prevented him from bleeding out from his wounds when he hit the ground.

I won't tell you I wasn't scared. I was. Ryan, my instructor, told me just before the door opened and we tumbled out—which in that first few seconds is like falling in a vacuum of pure shrieking insanity—that he could feel my heart beating above the vibration of the plane. He wasn't kidding.

But then, just as suddenly, we were flying, buoyant even, as if the air was pushing us back into the sky, and we were carving our descent in a series of controlled and rewarding turns. Fear vanished. It was true flight: loud, windy, with all of Central Oregon spread out beneath us in a vision of mountain lakes and forests and volcanoes holding snow in the lees. We could see St. Helens, Rainier, the raw power of the Cascade peaks marching off into the horizon, and far below, the little town of Sisters, looking something like a cartoon hamlet just recently hacked out of the forest.

And then the parachute opened and we began to float, the world gone so suddenly quiet it seemed we were drifting in the primordial. And there is nothing like hanging lazily under the canopy, taking in the curvature of a world you might never see again in the same way, and looking up to see your wife, still streaking earthward at 150 mph, free-falling in a pink flight suit.

We could do worse than to model something of our drive for life after David Beautiful Bald Eagle, who just kept living well when age and gravity and time might have forced him to close up shop. But he didn't allow that, and instead seemed to grow bigger and stronger with age. We should do so well. His example inspired us, and we were happy to shove complacency aside, widen the path, and just get after the good and sweet business of being alive.

So, this jump's for you, Chief Beautiful Bald Eagle. Walk on.

Bee Lives Matter

Historians and archeologists tell us that human beings began collecting wild honey about ten thousand years ago. Evidence shows up in ancient North African pottery, Egyptian art, and honey in jars has been recovered from the tombs of the Pharaohs. By six hundred BCE the Picts of ancient Scotland—naturally it was the Scots—were brewing honey ale, or mead, a legacy which comes down to us even in poetry such as the epic of Beowulf, which means bee-wolf, or bear.

But bees are not just a luxury because they make honey. They are necessity. They are required for an almond to set, for example, and the work they do is vital for any number of other crops we rely on but rarely think about when we tuck in for a meal. Bees are an engine for the success of many other species of life, and a bellwether for the health of our planet.

Sadly, the world's bees are not doing well. From Colony Collapse Disorder to pesticides and infestations of treatment-resistant *Varroa* mites, the world's bees are in big trouble.

So, here on the Figure 8, we've decided to try our hand at beekeeping. I've been attending the Tumalo Bee Academy, reading widely, talking to experienced beekeepers, and last Saturday we picked up our first nucleus colony of bees and brought them home.

The basic building block of a man-made beehive is the "super," where the frames are stored. It's possible to buy the supers and frames already assembled, but I wanted to build them myself because, like most things worthy of our attention, the more I invest myself in the intricacies of the hive and the life of our bees, the bigger the rewards become.

I placed our hive in a clearing among the ponderosas that dominate the Figure 8, on the remnants of the old Deer Ridge Road where Gary Tewalt and other Sisters aboriginals once hunted deer. I set up the box facing southeast, where the bees would be primed to enjoy full sun year-round.

When I opened the nuc I was, momentarily, amazed by the sheer number of bees inside. No one counts the bees, but best estimates put the numbers for a nucleus colony at about ten thousand bees: one queen, mostly workers, and a smattering of drones whose only glorious function in this world is to mate with virgin queens. Of course, the drones die a Shakespearean death in the process, abdomens ripped open, but their purpose on earth is fulfilled in the act.

These bees had come from Medford in the middle of the night and were, thankfully, in a good mood when I brought them home. I can admit to feeling somewhat ridiculous in a full bee-suit, and glad some of my less-repressed friends weren't around to provide a running commentary, but in the suit I was able to handle and examine the frames—and watch the bees at work—without worrying about getting zapped on my first full day of keeping bees.

By lunchtime Wendy and I had the bees installed, fed, and apparently happy in their new home. We stood watching them—utterly mesmerized—as they began to fly, precisely marking their new location by some miracle of evolutionary GPS—a bee can fly up to eight miles in one direction looking for forage—and by early afternoon the first bees had found their way into our yard and were scrambling around on the flowering dandelions.

I feel a tremendous responsibility for our bees. There is some miracle in them, some fascinating glimpse into industry without guile—only steady purpose and a commitment to the things of life.

I would be dishonest if I didn't admit to harboring dreams of honey, but this first-year honey can only be a bonus—my focus is entirely on nurturing a strong colony that builds up its own sufficient stores to survive a Sisters winter into next spring.

In the evening, as the light was drawing out of the sky, I went back to the hive and sat beside it for a long time. The vigorous comings and goings of midday, when we saw the first bees returning with bright pollen on their legs, were easing off as the last bees flew home in staggered waves. They came out of the forest in buzzing and random bunches, like formations of B-17s scattered after a mission over Europe, and disappeared into the hive.

It was truly a singular and transcendent experience, enough to inspire me to take a slow walk around our place with fresh eyes, as if I had never seen any of it before, and to stand beside the apple trees appreciating in some new way the marvel and promise of their bright pink and red blossoms.

I stood in our little orchard for a long time then, until a single cold drop of rain hit my thumb. And then I looked up into the clouds, watching the tall tops of the ponderosas brush against the disorganized sky, and I thought of Robinson Jeffers, the wild bard of Point Sur, who watched the world closely and in awe and who implored us all to remember: "It is only a little planet, but how beautiful it is."

The Gorgon's Stare

"The intelligence chiefs stressed that Russia was attempting to undermine Western democracies through its ongoing information war waged by humans and automated computer programs known as bots on websites like Twitter, Facebook, Reddit, and Google."

—*Time Magazine*

"As society becomes ever more computerized, the programmer becomes its unacknowledged legislator."

—Nicholas Carr

During the first week of January, 1812, "a great number of men armed with pistols, hammers, and clubs, entered the dwelling house of George Ball, a framework knitter of Lenton, disguised with masks and handkerchiefs over their faces." These men, following on the heels of numerous other similar attacks in the preceding days and weeks, proceeded to beat Mr. Ball, and "wantonly and feloniously broke and destroyed five stocking frames standing in the work shop, four of which belonged to George Ball, and one frame, 40 gauge, belonging to Mr. Francis Braithwaite, hosier, Nottingham."

The men were Luddites, and they were responding to the unnerving and disenfranchising appearance of automation in their lives, in the form of stocking frames for the knitting of textiles. This new technology, which the Luddites believed would eventually push them out of work and into poverty, also threatened the old orders of apprenticeship, and in the view of those blackening their faces and smashing frames in the night, it was an economic movement rapidly transforming into a revolutionary force.

But automation, and the efficiencies it provides for producers and consumers, and the profit it generates for business, generally wins the day.

Over time, many of the Luddites were hanged or sent away to penal colonies. Some were acquitted for lack of evidence. And though the figure of Ned Ludlam was probably a fiction, the Luddite Rebellion—which at one time employed more British soldiers than the fight against Napoleon—was a first manifest swing at resistance to industrialization and the encroachment of machines into the deeper reaches of daily life: employment, artistry, and traditional craftsmanship.

One of the greater realizations of the last century, and the early years of the 21st century, is that while technology evolves quickly—sometimes overnight—human beings are locked into an evolutionary framework of biology that is much, much, slower. And as our machine creations—from lawnmowers to supercomputers—seep ever deeper into our lives—beating us at chess, scheduling our days, influencing elections—many are rightly concerned that we are indeed becoming, as Marx wrote, merely "a living appendage of the lifeless mechanism."

That tension is real. It is also frustrating and dangerous, and it is terribly important to consider as we face questions about models of interaction with our own creations—particularly software—into the future.

One goal of global software companies is to create an environment of "pervasive assistance." We know that because Justin Rattner, chief technology officer of Intel, has said so. The long-term consequence of that is to make software's presence and manipulative influence in our life invisible. And when it becomes invisible it also becomes unquestionable, unconfrontable, and uncontrollable.

Another goal of software companies is to break down naturally evolved human behaviors meant to protect us from each other. No longer is TS Eliot's notion of "preparing a face to meet the faces that we meet," a normal human function and key ingredient of intelligent and planned survival. According to Mark Zuckerberg, founder and CEO of Facebook, "You have one identity. The days of you having a different image for your work friends or co-workers and for the other people you know are probably coming to an end pretty quickly. ... having two identities for yourself is an example of a lack of integrity."

The presumption behind Zuckerberg's statement is, in equal parts, ignorant, arrogant, and remarkable, and would render virtually every human relationship into a robotic exchange of algorithms mediated by software. Hence, Facebook. When stories are reduced to mere algorithmic readings of complex human emotion and environmental inputs, we will have succeeded in sucking the soul out of life.

Which Yuval Noah Harari, in *Homo Deus,* says has already happened. "*Homo sapiens,*" he writes, "is not going to be exterminated by a robot revolt. Rather, *Homo sapiens* is likely to upgrade itself step by step, merging with robots and computers in the process, until our descendants will look back and realize that they are no longer the kind of animal that wrote the Bible, built the Great Wall of China and laughed at Charlie Chaplin's antics."

Harari argues that human beings have an innate desire to achieve immortality, and that having evolved out of, or away from, beliefs in the divine, the human response in the modern era has been necessarily to seek immortality through science and technology. It is this desire, he argues, that underwrites efforts at cryogenics, genetic cloning, and the merging of technology with the human body and mind.

> *"The rise of modern science and industry brought about the next revolution in human-animal relations. During the Agricultural Revolution humankind silenced animals and plants, and turned the animist grand opera into a dialogue between man and gods. During the Scientific Revolution humankind silenced the gods too. The world was now a one-man show. Humankind stood alone on an empty stage, talking to itself, negotiating with no one and acquiring enormous powers without any obligations. Having deciphered the mute laws of physics, chemistry and biology, humankind now does with them as it pleases."*
>
> —Yuval Noah Harari

It isn't difficult to imagine what Rattner's "pervasive assistance" looks like because it's already here, and it is fundamentally changing how we live on the planet. Google Maps is an excellent example.

Say you are about to visit a city. Calling up a Google map on your phone or your computer will present you with a vision of the city that Google wants you to see—or thinks, based on an algorithmic judgment of your likes and habits, that you want to see.

Based on what you eat, certain restaurants will appear. If you buy books, a bookstore will appear. If you have searched for gas stations, they will appear, and so on. This sort of pervasive assistance is part of a trend toward "neuro-ergonomics" in software design, programs designed to integrate so seamlessly into our thinking that we hardly notice that we have ceded our own responsibilities for discovery to a software program.

This is a fine example of the degenerative effects of computer automation, which flies in the face of what science calls the "Generation

Effect." The Generation Effect tells us that the more work the mind must do the more work the mind is capable of doing.

And certainly we are in the midst of an unparalleled surrender of our own curiosity and pioneering awareness—seen all around us in the humorous form of people running into telephone poles or toppling into water fountains while rubbing their smartphones—as we cede the once-critical ownership of awareness and self worth to manipulation by a machine and its algorithms.

> *"We believe that we have built a perhaps limitless power of comprehension into computers and other machines, but our minds remain as limited as ever. Our trust that machines can manipulate to humane effect quantities that are unintelligible and unimaginable to humans is incorrigibly strange."*
>
> —Wendell Berry

Nicholas Carr, in his excellent book *The Glass Cage,* poignantly highlights the dangers of technology when he writes: "Automation severs ends from means. It makes getting what we want easier, but it distances us from knowing." And it is this distance from knowing that is the truly dangerous part of the equation. At its furthest ends, it can obliterate the knowing portion of the equation entirely, and nothing is worse that not even knowing that you do not know.

Automation, at this stage in its evolution, already touches every facet of our lives. Many analysts have attributed the wild market gyrations of early 2018 with "algorithmic manipulations of high-speed traders." Algorithmic-based trading strategies are programmed to respond within milliseconds to market conditions, far outpacing a human's ability to react competitively. When those algorithms are triggered, massive numbers of shares are bought or sold in a blink, and the market can quickly find itself beaten into a corner.

When, during the recent correction, I spoke to my financial advisor, I asked him if there was a certain Dow Jones number at which I should become concerned. His answer was revelatory: "It should probably be more of an emotional trigger than a specific number," he said, which I maintain is probably true but leaves my family vulnerable to the behaviors of predatory software in the grand scheme.

> *"Taking the misanthropic view of automation, Google has come to see human cognition as creaky and inexact, a cumbersome biological process better handled by a computer."*
>
> —Nicholas Carr

The idea of an emotional trigger to market conditions is one thing, but it also hints at the question of morality in machines, which is an enormous problem for software engineers. Carr points out the problems with programming, say, a driverless car, to understand the difference between a child chasing a ball into the street, or a small dog. How does the car react? What do insurance companies have to say about how the car reacts? How will our machines "calculate their way out of moral dilemmas"?

And of course there is the lingering question of LARs, or Lethal Autonomous Robots, which are probably the future of the battlefield, and who will need to make battlefield decisions of enormous complexity.

"The only way for robots to become truly moral beings would be to follow our example and take a hybrid approach, both obeying rules and learning from experience. But creating a machine with that capacity is far beyond our technological grasp," writes Carr. "Before that happens, though, we'll need to figure out how to program computers to display 'supra-rational faculties'—to have emotions, social skills, consciousness, and a sense of 'being embodied in the world.' We'll need to become gods, in other words."

And finally, Carr says, correctly, that "The first shot freely taken by a robot will be a shot heard round the world. It will change war, and maybe society, forever."

> *"Sex-Dolls Brothel Opens in Spain and Many Predict Sex-Robot Tourism Soon To Follow."*
>
> —*Forbes*

> *"Sex with humans could soon be a thing of the past."*
>
> —*Spiegel*

In the words of Arthur C Clarke, "We've designed a system that discards us." Which can already be seen almost anywhere we choose to look, and which was the original fear driving the Luddites to smash weaving frames and whose fears of displacement and unemployment were also finally realized.

At the current pace of development and disenfranchisement of human capacity, one might be forgiven for wondering at what point a modern version of the Luddites packs a van full of explosives and attempts to drive it through the gates of Google, or Apple, or Intel. It is interesting to realize that today's version of the truly dangerous underground radical is anyone—marvelous people like my wife, for instance—who makes a conscious choice to remain outside the pervasive and utterly controlling worldwide digital nervous system.

> *"The Robots are Coming for Garment Workers"*

> *"There's only one problem: most of the alternatives higher up the value chain, like electronics, are automating as well."*
>
> —*The Wall Street Journal*

I will only be surprised if that sort of modern Luddite Rebellion doesn't happen in my lifetime. I don't expect it to win out, but I expect that at some point it will begin to manifest, and I expect that in another century or two someone will be writing about the quaint little rebellion against software that happened way back when.

And that's another problem with pervasive automation because it will begin to erode our ability to properly interpret history. We will, I would argue, eventually be incapable of reproducing, or even understanding, the conditions of antiquity. We will find ourselves so far removed from similar day-to-day circumstances that our ability to interpret or understand the equations of decision-making in an untechnical world that we will essentially be looking at alien creatures.

To a large degree we do that already when looking at the bones and burials of our ancestors who, at this point, we still have far more in common with than future generations will have with us.

We spend a lot of time thinking about and interpreting the past, a necessary function to help explain how it is we have arrived at this particular point in history. But it occurs to me that I have not spent nearly enough time thinking about the future—except through a kind of emotional projection exercise while sifting through a maze of collated assumptions—and often with a kind of weighty dread that what is in the offing can only be terrifying.

I'm hopeful that thinking more about the future, and in particular the role of technology in that future, might in some way inform my desire to find a balance with technology as a tool and avoiding it as an inescapable crutch. Which it may very well become for our grandchildren, or their grandchildren, as software developers and engineers seek every day, inexorably, to combine the computer's contemporary omnipresence with a future omniscience.

"The value of a well-made and well-used tool lies not only in what it produces for us, but *what it produces in us*," Carr writes. We can see what pervasive technology produces *for* us, and some of it is extremely beneficial. But given that one in five Americans take either depression or anxiety medications, I think we also have a glimpse into what all of this pervasive technology produces *in* us.

We can guard against the designs of software engineers and futurists, if we are so inclined, by refusing to allow technology to become, what Carr describes "enshrouded in abstraction," and by resisting the trend of "inscrutable technology become[ing] an invisible technology."

Because, as Carr writes, "At that point, the technology's assumptions and intentions have infiltrated our own desires and actions. We no longer know whether the software is aiding us or controlling us. We're behind the wheel, but we can't be sure who's driving."

Sagebrush Sam and the Census Man

For several months I have been receiving letters from the United States Census Bureau demanding that I submit to a supplemental census exam. These letters have grown increasingly grim, advising me that my "response is required by law," citing the applicable U.S. Code, and carrying the implicit threat of prosecution. The letters have also told me—or rather, the "resident of said address"—that my failure to perform this obligation would also result in a visit from "an official" of the government.

I have thrown all of these demands, which don't even name me specifically—which is a "proof of service" fail, straight into the trash. I've given the government all of the cooperation I intend to give them in this lifetime—minus the obvious and distasteful yearly ritual of rendering unto Caesar what is Caesar's.

Yesterday afternoon I walked down to the barn and saddled the mare. I didn't intend to ride her, because we are still getting to know each other, and because no one has been on her back in a long time. But I wanted to get some leather on her, and ease her gently back into the world of service. So I brushed her, and said nice things to her, dressed her up in a hackamore, then eased the old Billy Cook up behind her withers.

As I was leading her out into the arena, I saw a strange, obviously governmental—think Ford Taurus—car in the driveway. Guess who?

One of the delights of Central Oregon living is the occasional outburst of sporadic gunfire in the woods, and it was during my summit with the government agent—who began by asking a series of questions I refused to answer—that someone, probably over toward Whychus Creek, began hammering failure drills with an AR. There is no mistaking the cadence of an AR in the hands of someone who knows how to use it. *Two to the chest, one to the head.*

The gunfire made the colt, who was still in his paddock, go happily bananas, further distracting the Census Man, and as he returned to the laptop cradled in his arm, he waded further into the list of questions I wouldn't answer: *How much was your last power bill? How many rooms in your house? What is your place worth? Do you own it outright? Were you employed by someone last week?*

None of your business, I reminded him.

As the questions continued, serenaded by echoing gunfire and a colt gone bucking and farting out into the trees, I looked long into the woods beyond the barn. Then I turned and told the Census Man, "You know, I think some of the Bundys just moved in over there last month."

His face went ashen.

The truth is, I'm no rebel, and I have no personal beef with this nameless agent of the empire who was sent on the ridiculous task of asking me even more ridiculous questions. Nevertheless, somewhere deep in the shooter's third full magazine, I explained to the agent that I was going to keep refusing to answer his questions, but sincerely wanted to make his day easier, and that perhaps I might meet him somewhere in the middle. That wasn't hard, given that most—if not all—of the empire's questions are answerable in the realm of public information. So I gave him just enough, but I made him work for it, and my honor was satisfied. I'm nothing if not reasonable.

But I was still standing there with the mare. So I decided, in that moment, just to ride her. She's no bronc, probably doesn't have even a single buck left in her sweet soul, but I was feeling a little randy myself. "Just a sec," I told the agent, as he was turning to leave. "This horse ain't never been rode," I said, "so if you don't mind waiting, when she blows up and puts me in the rocks, I will need you to call the ambulance."

I could see in that moment, as the gunfire continued somewhere out in the woods and the colt was running furiously up and down the fence line, that the Census Man was living in desperately uncomfortable skin. I paused for dramatic effect, uttered an audible prayer, then swung up on the mare. She stood rock-still, of course, but I looked at the agent with my eyes blown wide and let out a long, Oscar-winning sigh of relief. I looked at the agent sincerely. "By God that's a miracle," I said.

The agent was walking backward toward his car, stumbling in the cheatgrass, cradling his laptop like a child. "Mind if I go now?" he said.

I tipped my hat. "By all means," I said, turning the old mare away. And the Census Man was still watching when I touched her up into an easy trot, down the road and into the trees.

Lamentations

I was not comfortable around the tiger. To say otherwise would be a lie, and it is evident in the photo. I'm sitting a respectable distance back, with a strange, indecisive grin on my face. Much like a great white shark, a full-grown Bengal tiger does not have eyes that are inviting of trust and appreciation. Plus, it's a cat, a hungry one no doubt, and hungry cats are a known quantity of deception. But I couldn't resist getting in on a photo.

The tiger had been residing in a two-horse open-sided trailer in the parking lot of Soper's Casino, walled off from a terrified colt by sheets of plywood. When we pulled into the lot, a slush and mud concoction that citizens of old Deadwood would have recognized, I walked over innocently to look at the horse. Then I saw the tiger. Then I jumped two feet in the air, felt the claws of unadulterated terror and premium outback shock.

And what is the outback? That good country where all things are not just possible, but they often happen, sometimes with legendary flair.

Thirty minutes before discovering the tiger I was feeding out cows from an old flatbed Studebaker that I managed to pilot by virtue of starting fluid, a stream of cussing, and baling twine knotted around the steering wheel. I was on the back at 10 mph, flying by wire and kicking off bales to cows covered in ice. And when that chore was finished, my grandfather and I drove to the top of Montgomery Pass to have breakfast at Soper's Casino.

Soper's no longer exists, except in my memory: a wind-raked (elevation 7,167) truck stop and casino where I played 21 on day-work pay; and watched, one summer afternoon on a barstool, OJ Simpson's famous pursuit on the LA freeway system. It is now, like much of Nevada, fired, crumbling, ransacked, and returning to the earth.

But it reminds me of a country I hope we never lose. There is a lot happening in the Modern West, there always is, and sometimes—where we allow for it—it still resembles that land of limitless opportunity for the strange and unruly that once existed, at least in our imaginations, in our beloved Old West.

Today there is the Bundy thing—which carries the stigma of unfortunate and enduring seriousness. There is Burning Man, which exists on the opposite end of the spectrum. And there are still cowboys and rangers and bandits and shopkeepers. But I have a growing fear that that the brackets are closing in precipitously, that we are in danger of losing forever that openness and even recklessness which once defined us.

I think we might lament one day—privately or in print—the loss of our sense of utter outback, of the pure, or intentionally crazy, and of our ability to enjoy the eccentrics and the far-outs who live on the dead frontier. Each passing year we grow closer to completely assimilating and mainstreaming a wild country that hosted any number of opportunities for the bizarre, the original, and the unimpeded.

We have seen it changing, as we ourselves have changed, pinched perhaps by the pressures of modern life to conform into a largely homogenous—and subsequently uninteresting—brand of the species. We make gatherings to celebrate those things that define us even as we are losing them. Maybe we do that, without really acknowledging it, *because* we are losing them. I'm reminded of the Ghost Dance, born not far from where I was raised, and those desperate attempts to simply dance back into existence a dying way of life once enjoyed.

Still, I sing lamentations for what we might lose, and I am angry that the best I can do is concoct a kind of modern-day ghost dance, in pathetic paragraphs, against the tide of rigid and boring comfort that is becoming our shared experience.

Down the road from my grandfather's place was a perfectly legal Nevada brothel—Janey's Ranch. The hookers from Janey's used to meet us at the top of Montgomery Pass in the fall, when we herded cattle home from the great and empty reaches of the Basalt Range. They would gather with platters of food and drink on the highway outside of Soper's Casino, hoisting trays of margaritas and limes, brilliant in whatever revealing outfit best kept them warm in the wind, smothering the cowboys with smiles and best wishes, laughs, and bad jokes. They were having a lot of fun, and so were we, while the cows bawled and mothered up with their calves in bad skies and spitting snow. And that was the sum total of the contract. I'm not sure anything of its kind exists anywhere else, or ever will again, but it was modern then and it was real and it was precisely the unbridled outback I love the most.

Today, Janey's is also gone. The old sign on the highway—made from a gigantic boiler tipped over on its side and painted silver—now reads, in black paint: "Janey's Ranch ... CLOSED. BEAT IT" Still a message worthy of the plain-spoken West.

And what about the tiger?

Three months after my grandfather and I ran into this tiger, it mauled to death the man who knelt beside me in the photograph. I know that because my grandfather sent me, by U.S. Mail—the way we used to do—a newspaper clipping reporting the event. In the margins my grandfather had scribbled: "Told you so."

A Meditation in the Barn

I decided to write this morning down here in the barn, snugged up in the tack room near the horses and the hay and the barn cats.

My wife and I have managed to do a few things right, and this barn is one of them. Aside from a particular stretch of rimrocked desert in northwest Nevada—which I won't tell you about—it may be my favorite place in the world. The tack room is heated, I've got a two-burner stove with a chipped enamel kettle where I can make tea, and I've fashioned this perfectly functional scrap-board desk that suits me fine.

The tack room is a kind of personal think-tank. I can brush aside a few wood screws, old tubes of phenylbutazone, random scraps of leather, and daydream at ease amongst the saddles and four generations of well-oiled tack. I like to sit here and listen to the horses, or lean into the window and watch the dogs run circles around the henhouse while the wind shakes snow from the ponderosas.

It's not a terrible way to jump-start a day.

Or a New Year. Like many others, I don't do resolutions—which are largely a way of lying to ourselves, and later forcing a series of embarrassing excuses—but I do embrace an evolving series of long-range visions, and winter is a great time to indulge a few of them.

Increasingly, my thoughts and energies are focused on building a particular kind of life underneath the noise, a way of navigating where politics end at the edge of our front porch, where we gather more often with friends to feast and play music, where next summer's garden explodes in outrageous vegetables, and where the obnoxious and heartbreakingly beautiful colt in the third stall starts as balanced and strong as his promise.

It should be—but never is—as easy as that.

The first one—shedding politics like an old skin—is the hardest one, but I'd like to get there if only because it underwrites almost everything else. I'd love to pay more attention to raising great tomatoes than to which layer of government wants to tax me, tear up the Bill of Rights, or cajole me into yet another Faustian choice. I'd love to focus on flying lead-changes rather than think, even once, about how we've achieved a nation addicted to opioids and other pharmaceuticals, or ponder the endless geo-political games played by people we don't know, probably wouldn't like if we did, and most certainly would never invite over for a barbecue and a beer.

I say all of that in a dreamy way. I'm not at all sure how realistic it is, given my conceits and predilections. I'm more and more certain that our government is merely a faraway monolith, working feverishly, like Las Vegas, mostly at reducing the individual to an "imbecilic dipstick," in the words of Ellen Meloy. And I'd join Meloy in saying that Vegas and the federal government share another trait, which is a kind of honest and elegant fraud.

One of the finer things about being down here, aw-shucksing and pretending I'm "folksy"—a reader's criticism that I absolutely love—is that for a while I can also pretend that politics don't matter much. And that creates a wonderful illusion right up until one of the mares throws back her ears and squeals at the other one, or the cats leave a dead rabbit in the alley, or our oldest dog pees on a bucket to remind us all who is actually running this place. I can embrace those little reminders with a smile, because the flip side of folksy seems to be a constant and largely uninteresting anger.

Modern living—and maybe it's always been this way—wedges us into an endless series of contradictions, a narrow channel with a lot of sandbars, and I guess what I'm striving for in my quaintest visions of the New Year is to reduce that friction, wherever and whenever possible. I'm seeking a less mediated life. I want to love the bulldozer and the trees at the same time, without looking over my shoulder for the next round of mortars lobbed in from one angry insurgency or another.

Of course, we never know where any of this is really going. Just before the New Year I was honored to officiate a wedding for two old friends. It was a small and lovely ceremony underneath a gigantic cottonwood. We were lucky to get a break in the cloud cover and fabulous evening light. And not a day had passed before we learned that two other old friends were getting divorced.

The more I think about things, the more I begin to suspect that despite my best efforts, I don't have a single answer. Maybe I don't even want one.

So for now, in the quiet of this lovely morning, I'm just going to sit down here in the barn, listening to the horses eat, and sipping tea from an old Police Foundation coffee mug. I might even light up my pipe and fill the air with the sweetest smoke. I can sit here happily for a long time doing that.

And anyway, it's cold outside, truly, and there is always more work to do.

Acknowledgements

I have been fortunate to make some very good friends in this life. I owe each of you a profound debt of gratitude: Jim Cornelius, Gailmarie Pahmeier, Dominic Gerbo, Mary Szybist, Dave Hedges, Chad Hunt, Casey Smith, Kristin Shamordola, Bert Lambert, Dan Zappa, Dan McGrew, Ed Olsen, Lynn Woodward, and most of all my mother, Christine DeForest, who bought me books.

Craig Rullman

Craig Rullman is an award-winning journalist and weekly columnist for *The Nugget Newspaper* in Sisters, Oregon. A former police detective and veteran of the United States Marine Corps, Mr. Rullman is a graduate of the University of Nevada, and holds an M.A. from Northern Arizona University. For several years he was a working cowboy on the deserts of Arizona, California, and Nevada. He lives with his wife on the Figure 8 Ranch, in the shadow of the Oregon Cascades.

Smoke Creek Press

www.ingramcontent.com/pod-product-compliance
Lightning Source LLC
Chambersburg PA
CBHW030742110726
47900CB00008B/2423

* 9 7 8 0 5 7 8 4 7 0 9 1 7 *